IN MEMORIAM

A Guide to Modern Funeral and Memorial Services
Second Edition

Edward Searl

Skinner House Books
Boston

Editor: Brenda Wong
Editor, 2nd Edition: Mary Benard
Designer: Suzanne Morgan

ISBN 1-55896-407-X
Printed in USA.

10 9 8 7 6 5 4 3 2 1
05 04 03 02 01 00

Acknowledgments
"Song (4)" from *The Wheel* by Wendell Berry. Copyright © 1982 by Wendell Berry. Reprinted by permission of North Point Press, a division of Farrar, Straus and Giroux, LLC.

Excerpt from *The Prophet* by Kahlil Gibran. Copyright © 1923 by Kahlil Gibran and renewed 1951 by Administrators C.T. A. of Kahlil Gibran Estate and Mary G. Gibran. Reprinted by permission of Alfred A. Knopf, a Division of Random House, Inc.

Excerpt from "Dirge Without Music" by Edna St. Vincent Millay, from *Collected Poems*, HarperCollins. Copyright © 1928, 1955 by Edna St. Vincent Millay and Norma Millay Ellis. Reprinted by permission of Elizabeth Barnett, literary executor.

"Out of the Stars" by Robert Terry Weston, from *Hymns for the Celebration of Life*, Unitarian Universalist Association, 1964, and "The Great Peace" by Robert Terry Weston, from *Seasons of the Soul*, Unitarian Universalist Association, 1964, reprinted by permission of Richard Weston-Jones, Executor, Estate of Robert Terry Weston.

Excerpt from "People" from *Selected Poems* by Yevgeny Yevtushenko, translated by Robin Milner-Gulland and Peter Levi, S.J. (Penguin Books, 1962). Copyright © 1962 by Robin Milner-Gulland and Peter Levi. Reproduced by permission of Penguin Books Ltd.

The story cited in "A Family Scattering of Ashes" is reprinted by permission of Sylvia Savage.

Library of Congress Cataloging-in-Publication Data
Searl, Edward, 1947-
    In memoriam: a guide to modern funeral and memorial services / Edward Searl.—2nd ed.
      p. cm.
    ISBN 1-55896-407-X (alk. paper)
    1. Funeral service. 2. Memorial service. I. Title
BV199.F8 S43 2000
265'.85—dc21
                                        00-036569
                                            CIP

Dedication

I learned how to fashion funeral and memorial services in 1977 during an internship at the First Universalist Church in Syracuse, New York, where the Rev. Charles Howe was my mentor. Another intern and I asked Charles and two other Syracuse-area ministers, the Revs. Nick Cardell and Ray Nasemann, to give us an *ad hoc* seminar. In an afternoon they introduced me to a human-centered, psychologically sound, liberal religious tradition from which the services in this book are drawn.

I dedicate this book to Charles, Nick, and Ray, representatives of a rich Unitarian Universalist tradition that has led the way in creating new forms for a new day to deal with humanity's eternal story—the story of living and of dying.

CONTENTS

Introduction
to the
Second Edition

When I wrote *In Memoriam* seven years ago, I made available to a larger audience a spiritually rich and psychologically sound way of crafting final rites of passage. Generations of Unitarian and Universalist ministers had pioneered the human-centered services I adapted for contemporary sensibilities and needs. My book paid tribute to these colleagues and a shared liberal religious vision that religion will respond to and serve real human needs.

I anticipated that ordinary persons, in the midst of a crisis, might pick up *In Memoriam*, easily access useful information, make necessary and prudent arrangements surrounding a death, and use its resources to construct and even lead a service of deep human meaning and emotional satisfaction. I designed this book to encourage preplanning. I hoped it would serve as an extended meditation about death—how death fits into the scheme of a human life. I was generally aware of contributing to a movement that seeks to return dying and death to a rightful place usurped by an economy of death.

For nearly a hundred years through the mid-twentieth century, a funeral industry appropriated rituals of death. This industry sanitized and sequestered this hard but essential reality of human existence. This contributed to a cultural denial of death and resulted in businesses that often profited obscenely and, in the process, exploited the bereaved. We must continue to be wary of the negative influences of the industry of death, while we reclaim the humanity and rediscover the meaning of death.

With perspective, I better see how my little book fits into progressing trends of consumer reaction and spiritual enrichment. I further see how it reflects my own aging and mortality issues, emblematic of an aging generation and demographic bulge.

I have turned fifty. The concerns of *In Memoriam* have a reality for me now they did not have ten years ago. In becoming a student of death and its rituals, I have acquired realizations that changed my attitudes. These realizations further embedded me in my own liberal religious tradition, as I learned about a Romantic nineteenth-century "culture of death."

In particular, I developed appreciation for the "rural cemetery movement" and the role New England Transcendentalists—American Romantics—played in taking death into the sunlight and open vistas of nature. In this second edition I speak to these appreciations in a new chapter, "Rituals of Remembrance."

A decade ago I would have more cavalierly sanctioned the scattering of ashes. Now I offer counsel to inter ashes beneath a memorial or monument in a garden cemetery. Of course, this is not an absolute judgment. There are circumstances and attitudes that make scattering ashes the right choice for the deceased and survivors.

As with all issues, true choice means that all possibilities may be reasonably considered. This book continues to offer choices. The process of making your choice begins with an inventory of your values and attitudes which the following materials encourage.

We have more choices available now than even a decade ago. Advocacy groups have become more assertive and accessible, particularly via the resources of the Internet. The funeral industry responds with new procedures and products. At the same time consolidation and mergers have made funeral chains industry leaders as small or "ma and pa" mortuaries decline. Contrary to traditional economies of scale, consumer costs have not decreased with consolidations. As before, the consumer must be educated relative to what is typically the third highest expenditure of a lifetime—after the purchases of a home and an automobile. A traditional funeral, exclusive of burial costs, typically costs $5,500.

But the changes relating to life's final rite of passage have not all been driven by heightened consumer consciousness. Spiritual concerns have brought about changes, too. In this regard, I applaud a renewed domestication of dying and death. The hospice movement has led the way by providing resources and care that allow a terminally ill person to die at home. Now funerals and memorial services, including the visitation or wake, are leaving the commercial funeral home and returning to churches and even homes. This is certainly made more attractive by the increasing popularity of direct cremation. Bringing dying and death home affirms life in the face of death, and the visitation and service in a more domestic or less commercial setting become more personal.

There are even those who advise home burial and offer instructions through books and articles. While this is the extreme, I think it reflects the contemporary trend to reincorporate dying and death into our living—not to sanitize it or make it a taboo—but to meet it honestly and spiritually, that is humanly, and to provide the rights and resources to do so.

This new edition offers supplementary thoughts about reclaiming the setting of funerals or memorial services. I add a service, "Gathered by Love," for the special circumstances of perinatal and neonatal loss. A new chapter, "Rituals of Remembrance," considers the significance of monuments and memorials. The new edition contains several pieces to supplement the service scripts and to speak to particular circumstances: suicide, passive euthanasia, and cremation. The Appendices offer advice for personal planning and preparing an obituary.

Plans and Arrangements

Our culture has many taboos about dying and death. As a result, many people know little about something they will inevitably encounter—certainly in their own lives but likely in the lives of their family and friends as well.

This chapter provides basic information about the choices survivors must make, from the moment of death through the "religious" service to the burial or scattering of the ashes—the first phase of grief, which is marked by shock and disbelief. When death occurs, the survivors must quickly make a series of perplexing and difficult choices of considerable impact and long-lasting importance.

If you are informed about the choices and have thought about which ones you prefer, you will be better prepared. At the very least you will be an informed consumer. But a more important consideration is that you will want to adequately honor the deceased (or have your own desires honored).

The bereaved's initial reactions to a death set the tone for and begin the long process of working through grief. The earliest responses and actions reverberate and are magnified through time. If griefwork—which begins immediately after a death—is done well, it leads to a reconstructed life and a return to living, no matter how shattering the death was for the bereaved.

While you may have a difficult time doing so at first, the information in this book can help you get beyond cultural taboos as well as your own reluctances and fears about death. Then you can plan and make arrangements, feeling confident that you're doing the right thing.

The Wisdom of Making Your Own Arrangements

Although death is not a pleasant topic to deal with, there are two strong reasons for planning ahead and leaving a set of instructions for your survivors. The most obvious reason is that your wishes and integrity will be honored. A second and equally important reason is that it shows consideration and respect for your survivors.

Death always comes as a shock, no matter how well prepared the bereaved may think they are. The grief that results is the deepest and most demanding of all human emotions. The physical and emotional systems of the bereaved undergo a series of protective, defensive, instinctive reactions based on the primal flight-or-fight response. Often, numbness and a sense of slow-motion time alter thought processes and emotional responses. Despite the disorientation that grief brings, the next of kin must make a series of decisions for which they usually have no experience. For their welfare, consider the range of options available to you. Consider the pressures and stresses that your survivors will experience.

With these significant considerations before you, you may be persuaded to preplan and even prepay for the arrangements you want. Appendix A, Personal Plans and Arrangements, is a simple, convenient, and valuable way of leaving your instructions to ensure your intentions and to assist and protect your survivors.

This form lists the various options available at death. In addition to the basic choices of funeral or memorial service, burial or cremation, it has provisions for indicating the arrangements you have made for organ donation or for giving your body to medical research.

A Checklist

The following checklist outlines the customary order of arrangements to be made for someone who has just died.

1. Contact local clergy and attorney (before death if possible) to determine whether the deceased has left instructions.

2. At death (in a hospital) contact a funeral home, memorial society, or alternative funeral service to remove the body and initiate and prepare docu-

mentation. If death occurs at home, first contact a doctor or coroner to verify death and issue a death certificate. If the deceased was under hospice care, contact your hospice care provider, who will facilitate arrangements.

3. Decide if the body is to remain "in state" or to be cremated. (If cremation is the choice, embalming may not be necessary.)

4. Notify family members.

5. If there will be a traditional funeral, meet with the funeral director to purchase a casket, a vault, a cemetery plot, and other services associated with visitation, viewing, religious service, and burial.

6. Determine whether memorial flowers are desired or whether there might be a substitute memorial designation (such as a church or charity).

7. Set a time and place for the religious service with the officiant (perhaps clergy).

8. Arrange for a death notice or obituary to appear in the newspaper. The funeral director can do this, or you can contact the newspaper directly.

9. Gather meaningful memorabilia to display during the visitation and service.

10. Plan for a postservice reception.

11. Consider a long-term memorial as described in the "Living Memorials" chapter.

RECLAIMING THE SETTING

The growing popularity of cremation, particularly direct cremation, significantly increases the possibilities of where a memorial service may be held. Without a physical body to consider, the practical demands to use the facilities of a funeral home diminish. Therefore, you can opt for a setting more congenial to the memory of the deceased and fitting to your sensibilities.

An appropriate alternative setting for both the visitation and the service is a house of worship, a lodge, a community building, even a private residence. (As late as the nineteenth century, the body was often "laid out" in the home parlor of the deceased. The euphemistic names funeral home and funeral parlor hearken back to these earlier customs.) The ashes, in an attractive container, with photographs, memorabilia, candles, and flowers, may be arranged in an altar-like tableau to provide a focal point where mourners may pay their respects to the deceased and offer condolences to the bereaved. Such a setting is also congenial to a religious service that celebrates the life of the deceased and welcomes the attendees with refreshments and food, music, and special decorative touches that a traditional provider might discourage, if not prohibit, in a commercial establishment.

In the larger scheme of the cost of services, where the use of the funeral facilities and staff are add-on expenses, using an alternative setting does not save a great deal. What is gained usually has value relative to personal aesthetics. Supporting these alternatives are new boutique-like businesses that provide a full range of consumer goods related to funeral and memorial services— memorial and prayer cards, guest books, urns, and coffins, for example—that can be bought piecemeal by the general public. These businesses tacitly acknowledge adaptations the funeral industry must make to accommodate some more informed and creative consumers.

Nontraditional arrangements can aid in crafting services more celebratory than grief-stricken, though grief will not be neglected. Such arrangements may be seen as traditional because they revive ways of dealing with death in the home by the family that preceded the funeral industry, the origins of which date only from the Civil War era.

In preplanning, you might consider the message about living and dying you wish to leave with your survivors—how the setting of the visitation and service influence that message. If you are pressed by the circumstances of a death and must decide what to do, know that nontraditional options are not only possible, but appropriate and increasingly popular choices. The services in this book generally lend themselves to a more celebratory way of responding to and meeting death in friendlier, more domestic settings.

THREE TYPES OF RELIGIOUS SERVICES

Your choice of "religious" service will influence the plans and arrangements you need to make. A "religious" service is the gathering of family and friends to participate in an observance of words, and possibly music and simple ritual, to mark the initial phase of grief. It also marks the beginning of the long process of recovery and is the focal point of the events surrounding the death. Though it pays tribute to the deceased, the religious service also serves the living so that they can deal with, find the meaning in, and begin to get beyond death.

There are three basic kinds of religious services for death: the funeral, the memorial service, and the committal service.

Funeral

This is the traditional service. The body, in a casket that is open or closed, is physically present while the funeral service takes place. A funeral may be held in a funeral home for convenience, though it can also be held in a church, lodge, union hall, or even a private residence. Often the actual funeral service is preceded by a time of visitation, when family and friends greet one another in the presence of the casket. (This is also called the wake.) If the casket is open so that the body can be seen during the visitation, this is known as a viewing. Visitation or viewing may occur the day before or just before the funeral service. After the funeral service, the body is either interred (buried) or cremated.

A committal service, before the body or cremation remains will be interred, may or may not follow the funeral. If this is the sole service, it is commonly known as the grave-side service. (In the instance of cremation, the interment of ashes can take place days, weeks, or even months later.) Usually the committal service takes place at the cemetery. However, it may take place immediately after the funeral service in the same location as the funeral. Actual interment then takes place later at the cemetery without ceremony.

When there is a grave-side committal service after the funeral, a formal funeral procession of automobiles accompanies the body to the cemetery.

Memorial Service

This popular service takes place after the body has been buried, cremated, or otherwise permanently taken (as when donated for medical research). The memorial service may take place within a day or two of death, as in the case of a funeral. Or, depending on circumstances and arrangements, it can take place weeks or months after death. For the sake of "good" and normal grieving, however, the closer to the time of death the memorial service takes place, the better. The church is a frequent setting for the memorial service, but any appropriate site can be used, such as a public hall, a private home, or an outdoor setting.

Committal Service

This service usually takes place at the site where the body or the cremation remains will be buried. Sometimes the committal service is held in a chapel on the cemetery grounds. Less frequently, often during inclement weather, it is done at the end of the funeral in the same place where the funeral has been held.

The committal service can be the sole service and is usually briefer than either a funeral or memorial service. Whether or not the casket or urn is physically placed in the ground during this graveside service is a matter of choice. Some authorities believe that the experience of seeing the body or remains lowered into the ground has therapeutic value in the grief process.

Planning a Traditional Funeral

A hospital is the most common place for death, but more and more people are dying at home because of at-home hospice care. In either case, the immediate question involves the body. What is to be done with it?

The customary response is to contact a local funeral home for dealing with the body. The decision to embalm the body for visitation and possible viewing at the funeral home (though a church or social hall may also be the setting) is the first of many decisions. Each decision has its own cost, emotional as well as financial.

Within twenty-four hours after the death, the next of kin will visit the funeral home to purchase a casket. If the casket will be buried, a burial vault is usually required by the cemetery or by state law to encase the casket in the ground. Caskets are manufactured in a range of styles in both wood and metal. Even a plain, basic casket costs several hundred dollars. Modest caskets can cost several thousand dollars, while more elaborate caskets crafted out of quality wood and lined with silk can cost tens of thousands. Likewise, vaults range in quality from rough, relatively inexpensive, concrete shells to watertight, expensive, finished concrete containers.

People who are faced with choosing a casket and vault for a loved one after the first hours of death are among the most vulnerable of all consumers. In a state of deep grief and easily stirred guilt, the bereaved can be persuaded to make choices they would not normally make. Survivors must be careful at this time to make choices they will not later regret as having been too expensive or too ostentatious.

Once the casket and vault are purchased, survivors are then faced with the question of where the casket will be interred or entombed. Bear in mind that a cemetery plot, tomb, or crypt is costly, and the purchase price does not include the cost of "opening (digging) the grave" or the cost of purchasing and placing a tombstone or marker.

To these necessary fees for the funeral and burial add other expenses for the use of the funeral home's rooms, vehicles to the cemetery, and staff services.

A funeral home's services for a complete, traditional funeral are expensive. In response to these high costs, many funeral homes now offer prepayment options. Before you die, you choose the services you desire, paying a one-time fee that is held in a trust. Or you might purchase insurance or an annuity through the local funeral home. When death occurs, your survivors will have no decisions to make and no extraordinary out-of-pocket expenses.

In a similar way, cemeteries sell lots and mausolea or other spaces for future use. It is common practice to buy family space for husband, wife, and other relations.

In consideration for your next of kin, especially if you desire a traditional funeral and burial, you might choose a local funeral home and consult its funeral director about the services and products offered. Planning for, choosing, and prepaying funeral services relieve your next of kin from difficult and trying decisions, as well as protect them when they will be most vulnerable.

For many, using the services of a familiar and trusted funeral home is the right, though relatively expensive, choice for a variety of reasons. Its complete and thorough services grant peace of mind, while guaranteeing a standard of excellence consistent with your expectations.

ALTERNATIVE FUNERAL SERVICES

When planning and making your own arrangements, you may want to consider some alternatives to the traditional funeral home, especially if you live in a metropolitan area.

Memorial societies have been popular in this country since the 1950s. These not-for-profit consumer organizations can reduce the cost of a typical funeral by as much as 80 percent. By working with local funeral directors who are willing to make their profit on the volume of business they receive, memorial societies can offer such economical services. A standard funeral, including the services of the funeral director, removal of the body, preparation of documentation, embalming, visitation hours at a funeral home, a simple wood casket, and transportation to the cemetery, might cost $1,000 if it were arranged through a memorial society, compared to $5,000 for a service arranged through a traditional funeral home.

A nominal, one-time membership fee entitles you to use the economical and efficient services of your local memorial society. At death, survivors can contact the memorial society's office. The memorial society will then notify a local funeral director who will work with the deceased's family, providing whatever services are requested according to the memorial society's economical schedule of services.

More recently, so-called "alternative funeral services" operated as for-profit businesses have sprung up in response to consumers' demands for low-cost services. Some of these businesses specialize in cremation services only. Others offer a full range of services, from cremation to visitation at a funeral home to interment. These businesses may also require a modest membership or registration fee. They too offer prepayment options, including insurance, annuities, and trusts. Expect the cost of the alternative funeral services to be about half of what a traditional funeral home would charge for comparable arrangements.

The yellow pages are a good source for finding such alternative services in your area.

Preparations to Enhance the Service

In organizing a funeral or memorial service, certain preparations enhance the overall experience. In shaping your service, you will want to consider the following arrangements and additions.

Beginning and Ending the Service

A clear, decisive beginning and ending will relieve any confusion and anxiety on the part of the attendees.

Just before the service begins, immediate family members enter the room where the service will take place after everyone else has taken their seats. Seats in the front of the room have been reserved for them. The service leader(s) can enter with—even escort—the family and begin the service immediately after the family members have settled in their seats. If music is playing in the background beforehand, it should be ending as, or soon after, the family and service leader(s) enter.

To end the service, everyone can be asked to stand for the closing words or benediction. At the conclusion the family departs with the service leader(s) leading the way, signaling that everyone else may exit. A concluding musical selection can be played while guests exit.

Music

If the music is provided by the funeral home, you can usually choose (within limits) what will be played either on the organ or through the sound system. You can arrange for your own musicians—either hired for the occasion or people you know who play. You can also arrange your own selection(s) of recorded music. Consider the music that the deceased enjoyed, even if it is not traditionally funereal. Simple classical selections, especially piano and solo vocals, work well.

Flowers

In season, simple home-done arrangements can be more meaningful than elaborate professional arrangements. You can also request that those who wish to honor the deceased may make a donation to a designated charity in lieu of flowers.

Photographs

Either a single photo or a collage of photographs of the deceased through the years can be displayed in the room where the service is held. This type of display usually has good effect.

Memorial Designations

You may want to place information and appropriate envelopes for your designated memorial in a prominent place, for instance next to the guest register, the memorial cards, or the photograph display. Or have an usher/greeter hand out and collect the information sheets and envelopes. Common designations include medical societies, universities, churches, and special charities that the deceased supported.

Guest Register

Placed in a visible and accessible place, usually near the entrance to the room where the service is held, a guest register will be useful when the family wants to recall who came.

Ushers/Greeters

Not only can ushers/greeters welcome those who come, they can watch over and assist with any special arrangements. Instead of close family members, draw upon friends and neighbors to fill this role.

Announcements

The appropriate place to make a special announcement, such as information about a reception to follow the service, is before the closing words or benediction in the service. (If the reception will be held in another location, maps are helpful.)

The Rural Cemetery Movement

In preplanning and in attending to a death, it is worth considering the significance of cemeteries, especially those cast in the spiritual aesthetics of the rural cemetery movement. Cemeteries and similar places of interment serve the ongoing grief and remembrance needs of survivors. In this regard, do not discount your desires to leave a monument or physical memorial behind as a focal point and even as an ongoing contribution to our common world.

The cemetery is a relatively recent innovation. In the first half of the nineteenth century it replaced the graveyard—the traditional burying ground surrounding a church. The cemetery signified a revolution in how death was dealt with: a Romantic attitude concerned with Transcendental meanings, more naturalistic and humanistic. New England Transcendentalists, influential American Romantics, led the way in what scholars call the "cult of cemeteries," which marked a cultural shift.

Radicals of their day, American Transcendentalists viewed the walled graveyard as shadowed by the pessimistic theology of their Puritan ancestors. These Transcendentalists looked to the classical Greeks, who buried their dead outside their city, where for eternity they would be embraced by shading trees and soothed by murmuring streams. The Greeks called such a place *koimeterion*, which translates as "sleeping place" and is the source of the word *cemetery*. These burial grounds were also handy to the rural resorts where the Greeks studied philosophy and contemplated nature, thereby integrating death into a natural scheme.

In imitation, Transcendentalists in the early nineteenth century took death into the sunshine, fresh air, and open vistas of nature. Mt. Auburn Cemetery in Cambridge, a suburb of Boston, America's Athens, and near Harvard College, launched the rural cemetery movement in America in 1831.

Mt. Auburn immediately became a fashionable place to visit and influenced the popular culture of nineteenth-century America. It and its imitators artfully and spiritually sculpted landscapes and incorporated death into a natural order while stimulating acceptance and understanding.

Rural cemeteries were intended to serve as "schools of life." Through carefully designed grounds, nature taught its varied lessons. For example, the repetition of the seasons served as a window on the cycle of death and rebirth—if not of the individual, then of the generations.

The landscape architects who designed the early cemeteries incorporated a Romantic aesthetic in their cemetery schemes. Deciduous trees, including the evocative weeping willow, provided an emblem of the transience of life. Evergreens, the cedar in particular, testified that virtue cannot be destroyed, even by the most searing winter. Ponds, reflecting the sky, mingled the real with the ideal, as did the horizon where heaven met earth. Simple element joined to simple element created a solemn grandeur deliberately sublime. Vistas opened the eye to the borderline of the horizon and stimulated the spiritual imagination to Transcendental understandings—a liminal experience.

Being alive in the midst of the dead was itself a liminal experience. It evoked spiritual realizations. The Transcendentalists cultivated liminality—borderline experiences. The cemetery not only provided a setting for the borderline of life and death; to the reflective person it was perched on the borderline of time and eternity as well as the past and the future.

The rural or garden (as it is also known) cemetery, set in nature and sculpted to inspire spiritual realizations, quickly became the standard for American burial. Many of the great cemeteries of America to this day retain a strong sense of nature. They are oases of peace and even have become venues of recreation. (Mt. Auburn, for instance, is a haven for bird watchers.) The contemporary borderline of city and cemetery actually adds an additional liminal experience, one that the designers probably did not anticipate.

Though they are burial grounds, cemeteries are not morbid places to those who approach them with the attitude of the old Transcendentalists. They are intentional creations of sublime beauty that can evoke incredible meaning. Of course, some cemeteries are more successful in attaining the Transcendental ideals than others.

Similar to the Transcendental vision of the cemetery are memorial gardens and arboreta where cremated remains may be buried or scattered. Often a special planting signifies the deceased. This growing trend is an attractive adaptation of the rural cemetery ideal. An Internet search is a good way to find such innovative and natural memorial places.

As you begin to think about your own mortality and make arrangements regarding your loved ones and yourself, visit a local cemetery cast in the "garden style" and spend thoughtful time there. Consider long-lasting implications of interment and of erecting a monument in a suitable "sleeping place" to remain as a memorial to you and a reminder for your survivors.

CREMATION

Immediate cremation significantly simplifies the choices as well as the cost of a funeral. A funeral home, memorial society, or an alternative funeral service can arrange for removing the body, preparing the documentation, and conducting the cremation. Expect the cremation arranged by a funeral home to be more expensive than cremation arranged by a memorial society or alternative funeral service.

In basic low-cost services, the cremation remains (a few ounces of ash and bits of bone) are returned to the family in a cardboard or fiberboard container. A metal container or urn can be purchased at an additional cost. These "cremains" (as they are sometimes called) can be interred or placed in a niche at any time. Such arrangements are made with a cemetery or mausoleum directly, or you can engage a funeral director to make them for you.

Frequently, the family chooses to scatter the ashes in a location of special meaning for the deceased. (Local ordinances and laws govern the legality of scattering. However, when done discreetly, such private scatterings occur without legal intervention.)

Cremation need not be immediate. That is, the body need not be taken from the deathbed directly to the crematorium. The body may be embalmed for visitation and viewing (open or closed casket) as for a traditional funeral service. Following the funeral service, the body will then be cremated. Interment or scattering occurs at a later time.

Grief

Grief is the emotional response to loss. Bereavement is the loss of an especially significant relationship. The grief of bereavement, when death's impact first occurs, usually results in profound shock and some sort of denial. From these two basic responses other responses may tumble and spill: physical pain, confusion, disorientation, numbness, anger, guilt, uncontrollable sobbing and crying out, restlessness, nervous energy, and searching for the deceased.

These responses are instinctual. When you experience the death of a person close to you, the most ancient and basic flight-or-fight response is triggered. The various systems of the body mobilize, but there is nothing tangible to fight, nor is there any place to flee. This frustration brings on tremendous mental, emotional, and physical stress.

Sometimes, no matter how much the survivor intellectually "understands" and "accepts" the death, the other systems of the body have minds of their own. They cause the feelings of disbelief, of denial, of "this can't be happening, especially to me."

In the early hours and first few days of grief, the rituals and ceremonies of death have important roles to fulfill, serving particular functions in the grieving process. The religious service provides a focus: The preparations and arrangements absorb some of the bereaved's nervous energy and restlessness. The actual service provides a socially approved outlet for expressions of grief, especially crying. It helps reinforce the reality of the death. And it marks the end of the first phase of the grief process.

THE LONG PROCESS OF GRIEVING

The grief process, or mourning, involves acceptance and reconstruction. Accepting the death of an intimate brings the realization that life will never be the same as it was. Life for the survivor must be made anew—reconstructed, often without the linchpin that held that life together.

To be properly understood, grief must be seen as a loss for the survivors: the loss of what was normal, routine, comfortable, and secure—a way of life has ended with the death. Grief then becomes not so much grief for the deceased, but grief for the dislocation that death causes for the survivor. We grieve not so much for the dead person as for the parallel and much more intimate death of our own way of life.

The first phase of grief is shock. Shock is followed by a longer, sometimes extended, period of even more painful and intense feelings. The person who grieves will eventually sink to the emptiest and most despairing depths of personal being. Then, from these depths, if the person who grieves finds resolve and strength (and all persons who brave the depths of feeling have these means), a gradual and halting recovery takes place.

In its entirety, recovery and reconstruction, the latter phases of the grief process, may take months, a year, or several years. Usually, the more significant the deceased, the more painful and extended the grief process will be.

There is no right way to grieve, no recipe for proper mourning. Everyone must go through it according to her or his personal abilities and internal clock. However, there is a pattern of experiences, not so much distinct stages as a continuum, that many people who grieve go through.

Many helpful popular books describe the grief process based on contemporary clinical research. Conventional wisdom recommends that for true recovery to take place following a significant loss, the survivor must let the feelings flow, no matter how painful they may be, no matter how negative or destructive they seem. If there is anger at the deceased for dying, that anger needs expression. If there is resentment at life and its source for the scheme of things that makes death necessary, that resentment needs expression.

These intense, sometimes surprising, often conflicting feelings, compounded by the reality of the changes that death causes for the survivor, constitute the second phase of the grief process—the phase of intense psychic pain that leads to the depth and despair of personal being. From this rock bottom a transformation can take place and recovery can begin.

To be able to feel deeply and fully all the pain that is in the mind, heart, and soul when bereavement comes is one of the keys to successful grieving that leads again to life. Life will never be the same. But life continues and can once again be lived and even enjoyed.

The Importance of a Religious Ceremony

In this scheme the ceremony that marks the death—the religious service of gathered family and friends—looms large. It acknowledges real feelings and recommends a way of grieving.

The funeral and memorial services contained in this book have certain intentions:

1. to acknowledge the death, reinforcing its reality by pairing the name of the deceased with the factual statement that a death has occurred and a profound loss is being experienced;

2. to give permission and encouragement to grieve openly and deeply and also to allow disturbing and conflicting emotions to come to the surface and not be judged;

3. to speak honestly of the deceased in a eulogy so that the loss and intense feelings have a fair representation of their source;

4. to "do the right thing" for the deceased by having an appropriate and meaningful ceremony, while saying a final good-bye, letting the dead "rest in peace";

5. to affirm that life will continue and recovery will happen in time, even though the loss is enormous, if the death is openly acknowledged and the emotions are allowed to flow freely;

6. to declare that while life will never be the same as it was, it will be enriched by the memories and continuing influences of the deceased;

7. to counsel that death and grief are universal, timeless experiences; and though it may seem as though we are desperately alone when death confronts us, we are joined in one great empathetic human family.

This book recommends that you fashion the religious service—the ceremony of death—in meaningful ways, even if those ways are nontraditional.

Say words that speak to the reality of the event, words that speak to the heart and mind clearly and directly. Become involved by doing simple, meaningful rituals such as lighting candles, contributing a brief personal tribute, or adding a flower to a bouquet or a square to a quilt. Play music that the deceased enjoyed.

Regarding death ceremonies and the disposal of the body, there are no shoulds. No longer must we rely on tired and ineffective traditions and rituals that have lost their meanings. The only necessities, the only shoulds, are determined by the needs and desires of those who survive and grieve. When death confronts you, do those things that are especially meaningful and helpful to you.

You will find that the services in this book offer a structure for creative grief that touches universal, timeless, yet personal needs directly and honestly, with dignity, feeling, and beauty.

Traditional Ceremonies

The three major religions in the United States—Protestantism, Roman Catholicism, and Judaism—differ in the way they meet dying and death. The general approach as well as the services of this book, while humanistic and naturalistic, have their source in the Protestant tradition. In the arrangements you make in the face of death, you need to consider the expectations, understandings, and familiarities of the deceased's family and intimates.

The following sketches of the Protestant, Roman Catholic, and Jewish responses to death and grief outline each tradition's way.

PROTESTANT

Protestantism covers a broad spectrum of theology and practice embodied in a number of distinct denominations. Specific practices are associated with particular denominations. But generally speaking, there has emerged a Protestant style of dealing with death, which includes three elements: (1) the viewing of the body "in state" and "visitation" of the deceased's family; (2) a funeral or memorial service; and (3) a committal (interment) service.

Contemporary Protestant practices have been formed by a modern psychology of "good grieving," that is, a self-conscious reaction against a cultural denial of death. Thus, Protestant death practices have recently become more "confrontational"—open casket rather than closed, funeral rather than memorial service, and grave-side committal with the casket or urn lowered into the ground while the mourners are present are now more common.

Generally, viewing and visitation take place at the funeral home during specified hours. The coffin and the family are usually in the same room. A visitors book is signed. The family receives the visitors' condolences. The visitors may then pay respects to the deceased, physically standing before the casket and perhaps offering a silent prayer. A minister may offer an informal prayer service. Before departing, the visitor may then meet and greet others who have also come to pay respects. The length of the visit is generally brief.

The Protestant funeral or memorial service traditionally consists of readings from the Scriptures and prayers, with possibly a sermon or extended meditation to bring the Christian meaning of the occasion to the mourners. Many Protestant denominations do not include a eulogy, though music and singing are common. Contemporary additions to the traditional service include readings of poetry and prose, a sermon that is less evangelical and more therapeutic in its purpose, and a eulogy. The setting has historically been the church. Now the funeral home more often serves for both the viewing and the funeral service. In most instances the service lasts for a half hour.

The committal service is an even briefer service held at grave-side and includes Scripture readings and prayers. Under inclement conditions the committal service may take place immediately after the funeral service in the same location. Or the committal may be held in a chapel on the cemetery grounds.

Roman Catholic

The Roman Catholic tradition also includes three elements in its death ceremony: (1) a wake or vigil, (2) a funeral Mass, and (3) a burial ritual. There are certain variations of practice depending on ethnicity and region, but the Roman Catholic practices are prescribed by doctrine and tradition.

The wake is the vigil kept between the time of death and the funeral service and in former days was held in the family home. The family kept vigil around the clock near the prepared body, receiving guests and praying. Now the wake is held in a funeral home with specified hours for calling. During the wake, there might be a recitation of the rosary or a prayer service arranged by the parish priest. The family receives the condolences of the visitors. The visitors pay their respects to the deceased, who lies either in a closed casket or "in state" in an open casket.

The funeral service begins at the funeral home, where the family assembles to escort the casket to the church. The priest meets the casket at the entrance, covering it with a white pall. After an opening statement, the casket is brought to the front and a paschal candle is placed at the casket. A liturgy of the Word, including Scripture readings and a homily, is offered. Then a liturgy of the Eucharist is said and communion is served. A Rite of Commendation concludes the funeral Mass.

The burial rite is brief. It includes a blessing of the grave, Scripture readings, and prayer. It has provisions for additional readings and responses. The family often chooses to see the casket physically lowered into the ground.

According to the Decree of the Second Vatican Council, which is the Rite of Funerals that prescribes Roman Catholic practice, "The bodies of the faithful, which were temples of the Holy Spirit, should be shown honor and respect, but any kind of pomp or display should be avoided."

Jewish

Jewish tradition begins to deal with death before the actual event. If they are able, family members keep a bedside vigil. During this time, the person who is dying is encouraged to offer a personal confessional in keeping with confessionals offered at major life transitions, as well as on the Day of Atonement. The *Shema* is recited in the last moments as an affirmation of God and as comfort to the dying.

One becomes a mourner (*Ovel*) upon the death of either a father or mother, husband or wife, son or daughter, or brother or sister. Certain rituals are practiced by mourners. They traditionally rend their clothes (*Keriah*), which is now done symbolically by cutting a black ribbon and wearing it above the heart. The black ribbon is worn during the seven days of intense mourning (*Shiva*) when the mourners stay at home and receive callers. The lighting of a *Shiva* candle immediately after returning from the cemetery serves as a symbol of the divine presence. A "meal of recuperation," prepared by the community, welcomes the mourners home from the cemetery.

During the thirty days of mourning (*Sh-loshism*) that follow the seven days of *Shiva*, regular activities resume but places of entertainment are avoided.

Formal mourning ends after *Sh-loshism*'s thirty days, except when the death of a parent occurs, in which formal mourning lasts for a year and includes

Sabbath services and devotional recitations of the *Kaddish* prayer, now by women as well as men.

The yearly anniversary of death (*Yahrzeit*) is marked by the recitation of the *Kaddish* in the synagogue and the lighting of a special candle.

Thus, in Jewish tradition there are (1) three days of immediate and deep grief, ending with a funeral service and burial, (2) seven days of formal mourning, (3) thirty days of gradual renewal and return to life, and (4) eleven months of remembrance and recovery.

The Jewish funeral emphasizes the reality of death. The casket is present and prayers are offered, often including the Twenty-third Psalm. In the recitation of the *El Molay Rachamin*—a memorial prayer meaning "God full of compassion"—the deceased is included by name for the first time. A eulogy (*Hesped*) is also offered, honoring the deceased in truth and love.

After the funeral service the mourners form a procession to the cemetery for the burial service, at which the recitation of the *Kaddish* draws all into the universal community of mourners from which no one is excluded. Mourners often toss dirt on the casket after it has been lowered into the earth.

DISTINCTIONS

The death practices of Judaism emphasize community and continuity. Through the mourners' ritualized obligations, the whole community is assured that the deceased has not died alone (so when others also die, they too will not be alone). By its ritualized practices Judaism sets boundaries to grieving, conveying the message that, while necessary, grief must be contained and must lead the mourner into living a normal life once again. Yet the yearly remembrances confirm that the dead will not be forgotten. Judaism's direct dealing with dying and death has many elements of what is now recognized as psychologically healthy behavior. Dying and death are woven into community life, but they are also the "responsibility" of "designated" mourners for whom the ritualized mourning is therapeutic.

In the Roman Catholic tradition, the Paschal mystery—the death and resurrection of Christ, which assure all baptized believers of eternal life—is the focus of the funeral Mass. In keeping with the modern understanding of the needs of the mourners, the Vatican Decree instructs priests to also "consider the deceased and the circumstances of his life and death and be concerned also for the sorrow of the relatives and their Christian needs." Generally, Roman Catholics are counseled to meet death with faith, tradition, dignity, and simplicity.

The Protestant tradition, in all its diversity, approaches dying and death as a mystery that no one fully understands but that always causes self-reflection and soul-searching. In its more conservative denominations, Protestantism recommends that death be met with faith and often serves as an opportunity to evangelize. Many believe that traditional Protestantism, long the American cultural norm, has led to a cultural denial of death. As a result, dying and death have been significantly sanitized and distanced from personal experience through the arrangements of the hospital and the funeral home. Through contemporary psychology and theology, modern Protestantism seeks to reintegrate dying and death into personal experience. The needs of the grievers receive considerable attention in the arrangements of the minister to ensure that death will be a meaningful experience, eventually leading those who mourn back to living and life.

The Memorial
Service

You have the responsibility of organizing a funeral or memorial service for someone who has just died—most likely someone whom you loved and whose death has profoundly affected you. You must make quick but momentous decisions—decisions that touch the varied sensibilities of many people.

Where do you turn? What do you do? You might contact clergy of the deceased's faith, if the deceased had an affiliation. If this first option is not feasible, you might contact clergy from your religious tradition if you have an affiliation. Or you might seek out an available and generic sort of religious leader to organize and lead a service. These options may or may not provide you with the sort of service that will satisfy you by honoring the deceased and addressing the needs of those who will attend the service.

You also have the option of designing and leading your own service, especially if you want a service different from a conventional or stock religious service. You may want a service that speaks more to actual emotions—one that honestly and lovingly remembers the person who has died, that affirms through realities rather than through faith or dogma, and that is more participatory.

Using the resources in this book, you can lead a totally acceptable and satisfying funeral or memorial service of this more personal sort.

If you want to follow this option, read the marginal notes at the beginning of each of the following services. Decide which service suits your situation the best and read through it. (It helps to read it aloud, if only to yourself.) The marginal notes throughout each service will alert you to special arrangements for materials and speakers or offer suggestions for personalizing the service.

If you want to include a more formal eulogy, see "The Eulogy" for some tips. This section also includes actual eulogies to get you started.

Finally, you must decide what to do after the service has concluded. Some possibilities and recommendations are offered in the last two chapters.

The task before you—organizing and leading a service to observe a death—though difficult, will prove especially rewarding to you and to those who attend the service. These resources will take you through the steps of a successful service, but what results will be much more than the reciting of a formula. You will help create a personal and memorable conclusion to a human life that honors the deceased, confronts death, speaks to deep emotions, and leads to life.

Joy and Woe
Are Woven Fine

AFFIRMATION

A human life is sacred.
It is sacred in its being born.
It is sacred in its living.
And it is sacred in its dying.

INTENTIONS

The Sorrow and Joy of Life weave a tapestry of our individual lives as Death gathers us once again into a blessed community:

- to bid one we have known and loved, farewell and adieu;
- to search for Life's deepest meanings;
- to seek the comfort and the healing women and men offer one another;
- to say "yes" to Life's greatest expression—Love. Love believes all things, hopes for all things, endures all things. Love never ends.

At this time we are united with the wisdom and customs of all people in all ages. Though we are a small group of family and friends, we feel the embrace of the ageless human community. Though we are just a few, our strength and our resources are great, for they come from the deep well of all humanity. And in this spirit we join our individual feelings and thoughts as well as the faiths that sustain us separately into a harmony of Remembrance and Affirmation.

This is the most substantial and complete of these services, developing themes of community, grief, affirmation, death's meaning, paradox, remembrance, and thanksgiving. Its phrasing is more traditionally poetic; its cadence is more subdued. It suits a relatively larger, more formal gathering particularly well.

We shall celebrate _____'s living and we shall grieve _____'s dying because we know the truth of William Blake's words:

> Joy and woe are woven fine . . .
> Under every grief and pine
> Runs a joy with silken twine.
> It is right it should be so
> [We were] made for joy and woe.

Today we must grieve _____'s death. But we must also celebrate _____'s life. Though our grief is strong and we must mourn, we will not let the shadow of death obscure the living person who touched us many times, in many ways, filling our lives with memories, meaning, and love.

Let us be wise enough and let us be brave enough, this [morning/ afternoon/evening] to honestly remember and bravely celebrate a human life— the life that was _____'s life.

> So we have come together.
> It is good that we have come together,
> Because we need each other
>   in empathy and consolation,
> And because we need each other
>   in courage and wisdom:
> To face _____'s death,
> To celebrate _____'s life,
> And to show our love and support for _____'s family:
> _____
> Those who knew _____ best and loved [her/him] the most.

> It is good—right and fitting—that we have come together,
> Because a human life is sacred
>   in its being born,
>   in its living,
>   and also in its dying.

MEDITATION

Let the faiths and philosophies that sustain us separately meld into a unity of the most human and of the universal, where differences dissolve in the awe-inspiring yet wonderful harmony of the moment.

Before the wonder of living and dying we are humbled. In the midst of our sorrow and grief we feel a river of sacredness. Out of our memories and unending affections flows a thanksgiving. In our gathered concerns and compassion, healing begins.

Let the gifts of courage, wisdom, and thanksgiving come to each of us and swell among us today and in the days to come. Courage to face _____'s death. Wisdom to speak openly and honestly of our loss. And thanksgiving for _____'s life.

PONDERING DEATH'S MEANING

As conscious and self-conscious life, we know that death is inevitable. We know too that death shapes our life. Most of the time we can accept death as an abstract principle—a dispassionate fact of Life, part of the biological chain of generation begetting generation.

But when death becomes personal through someone we have known, respected, and loved, it comes in a variety of guises and triggers varying emotions.

When death comes to one of many years [as it has now], our grief is a quiet sadness.

When it comes to one who has suffered or endured a long [and painful] illness [as it has now] our grief is softened by a sense of welcome and even blessed relief.

When death comes suddenly—out of time, with little if any warning [as it has now]—our grief is sharp and shrieking.

No matter what guise death wears, we, being human, will "rage, rage against the dying of the light," as Dylan Thomas writes. Do not be perplexed by a gentle or savage rage you might feel now. Such a rage comes from a deep and universal human grief that living means dying. And do not be perplexed by other emotions that might rise unbidden from the depths of your being. You may feel a steady anger, rather than a bursting rage. (We do not easily relinquish to death those we love.) You may feel remorse, or worse, guilt for things you neglected to say to or do for the one who is dead. (At such times we more clearly see ourselves as relational beings.) You may fantasize about how things may have turned out differently. (What if this? What if that? And you torment yourself with maybes, shoulds, and if onlys.)

You may be harboring even more disturbing emotions. You may feel abandoned. You may in this death remember hurts and wrongs not resolved with the deceased.

Do not deny such emotions and their like. Accept them. Try to understand them. They are doors into Life's deeper understandings.

Death always brings us face to face with Life. There is opportunity in this moment and there is the means to begin to live Life again, though hesitantly, slowly at first. From this moment on, our living and doing can be more virtuous and more abundant. This is one of the paradoxes of such an occasion as this that it opens us to Life and living. And this paradox speaks volumes about the human condition.

> It is a miracle,
> Nothing less than a miracle:
> That flowers bloom every spring;
> That living thing begets living thing;
> That we human beings emerge
> Again and again
> > from ignorance to knowledge,
> > from hopelessness to meaning,
> > from sadness to joy.
> It is a miracle,
> Nothing less than a miracle.

Affirmations

We have suffered a deep loss, a grave loss. We can never fill the void caused by _____'s death. Before this emptiness we can only assert that love never ends. Our dead are immortal because we have loved them and they have loved us. Our dead live on through and in us: in the ways they have influenced and shaped us, in our memories of them, and in our flesh.

Trust that your memories and the passing of time will lessen your grief. Even the sharpest and deepest grief will become bearable, giving you the means and leading you to the desire to live on.

Nevertheless, it is also true that each of you who lived in _____'s special affection has also died some. But know that through _____'s life you have also been given life. You are more because _____ lived.

Let us all be strong in the conviction that in spite of death, the scheme of Life is ultimately good and that we must leave this service determined to live through the loss and the grief to an even more abundant Life.

We affirm:

> Death is not too high a price to pay
> for having lived. Mountains never die,
> nor do the seas or rocks or endless sky.
> Through countless centuries of time, they stay
> eternal, deathless. Yet they never live!
> If choice there were, I would not hesitate
> to choose mortality. Whatever Fate
> demanded in return for life I'd give,
> for never to have seen the fertile plains
> nor heard the winds nor felt the warm sun on sands
> beside the salty sea, nor touched the hands
> of those I love—without these, all the gains
> of timelessness would not be worth one day
> of living and of loving; come what may.
> —Dorothy N. Monroe, "The Cost"

REMEMBERING

Now we pause:
- to gather our individual feelings and thoughts;
- to remember the [woman/man] that was; how [she/he] touched our lives and our lives touched [her/his] life;

- to meditate upon the meaning of this occasion;
- to say our private farewell.

[With music/In silence] we enter into this time of personal memory and meditation.

EULOGY

(See "The Eulogy," beginning on page 99, for suggestions.)

AFFIRMATION

Death has brought us together, the death of _____. Yes, but also, no. Life has gathered us, too—Life channeled through _____'s life. And Love, Life's purest expression which survives even death, has gathered us—love for _____ and love for those who mourn _____'s death the most.

This occasion brings us to the edge of the abyss that threatens all we value with meaninglessness and oblivion. But it also opens Life to us. This moment is filled with the meaning we have brought to it through our shared grief, and through our concern and love for one another. In _____'s death we have found one another and have discovered the blessed healing men and women can do for one another.

MEDITATION

We give thanks for the life of _____. We remember [her/him] for the [woman/man] [she/he] was, though we can only know a portion of [her/his] world. [She/he] lives on through all [she/he] touched—the common Life of which we are all a part. [She/he] lives on, especially through those whose lives were intertwined with [her/his] life.

We remember those who love _____ the most and feel [her/his] loss the most: _____.

May they be granted the gifts of wisdom, courage, and thanksgiving that will give them forgiveness, acceptance, and peace.

And now as we say a final farewell to one we held dear, let us be comforted and trusting that a human life is full of meaning and purpose, even in death.

For a human life is sacred.
It is sacred in its being born.
It is sacred in its living.
And it is sacred in its dying.

BENEDICTION

Please rise, as you are able, as we conclude this service of Remembrance and
Affirmation for the life of _____.

> Humbly we stand in the face of death.
> Confidently we stand with Life.
> Our strength is the strength of many. Indeed, it is the strength of
>   all humanity throughout all time; because we share one fate and
>   a great compassion.
>
> May understanding go with us and peace, too, that we may live
>   together in charity, compassion, peace, and joy. In this spirit
>   let us—individually and together—go forth to live and to love.

Memory and Affirmation

AFFIRMATION

To our friends and loved ones we shall give the most worthy honor and tribute if we never say nor remember that they are dead but rather that they have lived; that thereby the . . . force and flow of their action and work may be carried over the gulfs of death and be made immortal in the true and earthly life which they had worthily used.

The dead are not dead if we have loved them truly. In our own lives we give them immortality.

Never are our loved ones so powerful to influence and inspire us then as after death has withdrawn them from us. Then we feel with a new intensity the elements of sweetness and love in their lives. Then they take their place like stars in a region of purity and peace.

—Stanton Coit, from *Services of Social Worship*

MEDITATION

We join our minds and hearts in an opening meditation:

For thoughtful, conscious life all creation is precariously contained in a mended cup of meaning. It is the cup from which we drink our lives—the cup with which we drink to life. It is a cup which is broken and mended, broken and mended over and over again. Each time an era passes, a way of life is destroyed, or someone of significance to us dies, we cry out that our cup is broken, and so it is. Yet, somehow—together—we must find, we do find the way to mend it all over again.

This service uses selections from a number of liberal clergy, especially Unitarian Universalists, who have pondered death's meaning and said yes to Life—the life of the deceased, the community life of the gathered women and men, and the ongoing life of generation following generation. It has a particularly thoughtful tone.

Now we are faced with that task of mending once more.
—Nick Cardell, "Cup of Meaning"

COMMUNITY

When a good person dies, family and friends gather for many reasons. Life has touched them with deep grief and they need one another's company for their own comfort. Just to be together, to look in friends' faces and see the common expression of hurt takes away the loneliness of their feelings and draws their hearts together in the blessed healing that men and women can do for one another.

At such a time the various faiths which sustain us separately come together in a harmony which acts across all creeds and assures us of the permanence of goodness, the inspiration of dedication, the value of a serviceable human life.

—William B. Rice, from *Great Occasions*

WE ARE GATHERED

We are gathered here this [morning/afternoon/evening] by death, the end of a good person's life—the life of _____. Though we will mourn, for mourn we must, let this also be a time for remembering the person [she/he] was, and let this be a time for affirming the kind of life which [she/he] lived. Let this, then, be not so much a time for brooding upon [her/his] death, but a time for celebrating a human life, the life that was _____'s life.

How true are the words of Kahlil Gibran who wrote:

When you are sorrowful look again in
Your heart, and you shall see that in truth
You are weeping for that which has been
Your delight.
—from *The Prophet*

By our presence here this [morning/afternoon/evening] we pay tribute to the memory of one who was an important part of our lives, who was dear to us, to show our love and respect for the person [she/he] was. And we have come together to show our love and support for _____ 's family: _____.

Their loss of _____ is sharp and deep, we know.

And so we have come together.
It is right and fitting that we have come together;
For a human life is sacred.
And so is its ending.

Three Gifts

It is my hope and heart's desire that we will be granted the coping and healing gifts of strength, courage, and wisdom: the strength to endure the pain of so sudden and so great a loss; the courage to speak openly to the loss; and the wisdom to give thanksgiving—thanksgiving for a life that touched and filled our lives.

Eternal Spirit of Life and Love, grant these gifts today and in the long days ahead. [Amen.]

Finding a Meaning

We know and accept, as best we can, the fact that death must and will come inevitably, to each and everyone. Death, we know, has several faces. When death comes to the aged or ill, it is often seen as an end to suffering. It is even welcome, and then our grief is a quiet sadness for a long life lived through to its final unfolding. However, when death comes [as it has now] to one in the fullness of life, we will, as Dylan Thomas describes, "rage, rage against the dying of the light." This death is not easy to accept, for we not only measure the greatness of our loss, but we think of what *might have been* for _____, and for us, had not death come like a thief in the night.

Our clouds of grief are hammered by disturbing and perhaps conflicting emotions. There is anger, for we do not easily give up our beloved. There is frustrating fantasy—if only this, or if only that. There might be guilt, too, and we punish ourselves for things left unsaid, or acts of courage and trust omitted. These emotions or their like, may swell and sweep over us. Do not deny them.

Accept them. Try to understand them, for they contain secrets to Life's meaning. In the final analysis, let us remember these words:

> All that we really know is that we stand here face to face with tragedy— universal, deep, and unending tragedy—tragedy that passes from time immemorial, to this moment, on into the future—tragedy that brings us to a sudden comprehension of ourselves as transient shadows on the screen of life.
>
> We shall never fill the place which has now been vacated, at least not in the flesh. Against such a void we can only exert courage and have faith in the knowledge that time does heal and memories do soften the wounds of so great a loss. But in the spirit, yes, in the spirit, that place is not emptied. The force that animates this continuing immortality is love: it is because they loved us and we them that our dead remain an immortal presence. Indeed, we must believe that whatever we have known and loved is ours, that whatever we have loved becomes a part of us, interfused with our lives, blended with mind and memory, joined to our souls. The dead are not dead if we have loved them truly. In our own lives we give them immortality.
>
> In this death it may be said that all of you who have lived in _____'s special affection have died a little, but in [her/his] life you have also found a richer and more abundant life.
>
> My hope, yes, my prayer for each of you is that you will go on strong in the faith that despite death, life is somehow good, even though we do not understand its mystery or its way.
> —Paul Carnes, adapted from memorial service
> delivered March 20, 1979

So in the face of this enormous death we affirm life: the goodness to be found in living and loving; the goodness to be realized in and through another life like our own—a life that grief presses strongly upon our thoughts and feelings just now.

A Personal Moment

Now let us pause to gather our individual feelings and thoughts, to meditate upon the meaning of this occasion, to offer a prayer, and most of all, to remember—each in our own private chamber of thoughts—the [woman/man] _____ was and the many and varied ways [her/his] life touched our lives. [In silence/With music] we enter a quiet and personal time.

Eulogy

(See "The Eulogy," beginning on page 99, for suggestions.)

Consolations

In opening I said it was death that brought us together. Yes, and no. For we have also been brought together by life, _____'s life that touched each of us in some way. And we have been brought together by Life's greatest expression, Love: love for _____ and also love for [her/his] family.

This occasion brings us to the edge of the abyss of death. But it also opens Life to us. This moment is filled with the meaning we bring to it, a meaning that has swelled this day among us through our shared grief, but more through our concern and love for one another. We have found one another and have discovered something of the blessed healing that we can do for each other.

Let us be mindful of those who bear the greatest burden of grief for _____'s death: [her/his] family, especially _____.

Our hearts reach out to you, and we find ourselves feeling deep within that which is beyond words. Yet, let these words presume to speak the unspeakable. We who are here, and those who are absent and thinking of you now, feel for you and offer our love so that you are not alone at this time of great loss.

Thanksgiving and Farewell

We have come together as a community of family and friends. We have suffered a hurt, a sudden and tragic loss. We have begun here to relieve that hurt, to acknowledge that loss by this service in which we celebrate the sadness and the joy with which our memories of _____ are enriched. How true are the words of the poet we heard earlier:

> When you are sorrowful look again in
> Your heart, and you shall see that in truth
> You are weeping for that which has been
> Your delight.

We give thanks for the life of _____. And we give thanks for [her/his] ways that made this community a better place to live and for [her/his] friendship, concern, and love that filled our lives.

May we who mourn _____'s death be granted the gifts of understanding and acceptance, and may we truly find our sense of thanksgiving—thanksgiving for a good, virtuous life lived fully and fruitfully.

We give thanks that _____ was—and is—a part of our common life. The truth of [her/his] life endures, for it is woven into the fabric of the larger Life of which we and _____ are all a part.

And now, as we remember and say a final farewell to one held dear, let us be confident and trusting that a human life is full of meaning and purpose, even in death.

> For a human life is a sacred thing.
> Its beginning is sacred.
> Its span of years is sacred.
> And its ending, its ending is sacred, too.
> Let _____'s name be inscribed on the Tree of Life, forever.

BENEDICTION

Please stand for these closing words and benedictions.

> We are gathered in the presence of a deep and abiding mystery; with humble hearts we bow before the veil which has fallen between us and the one we loved.

Let none fear: for greater than sorrow is love, which endures through pain and conquers even grief. Love binds all hearts in bonds of fellowship and courage. They who love unselfishly face even the depths with courage, for their strength is the strength of many and their courage rests upon the love of friends.

—Robert Terry Weston, from *A Cup of Strength*

And now may the peace which passes understanding,
The peace which comes with acceptance and thanksgiving,
The peace of the Spirit which rises above all the strains of the earth—
Be and abide with us all,
Both this day and forevermore. [Amen.]

The Counsel
of Nature

Out of the stars in their flight, out of the dust of eternity, here have we come,
Stardust and sunlight, mingling through time and through space.
>   Out of the stars have we come, up from time;
>   Out of the stars have we come.
Time out of time before time in the vastness of space, earth spun to orbit the sun,
Earth with the thunder of mountains newborn, the boiling of seas,
>   Earth warmed by sun, lit by sunlight: this is our home;
>   Out of the stars have we come.
Mystery hidden in mystery, back through all time;
Mystery rising from rocks in the storm and sea.
>   Out of the stars, rising from rocks and the sea,
>   Kindled by sunlight on earth, arose life.
Ponder this thing in your heart; ponder with awe:
Out of the sea to the land, out of the shallows came ferns.
>   Out of the sea to the land, up from darkness to light,
>   Rising to walk and to fly, out of the sea trembled life.
Ponder this thing in your heart, life up from sea:
Eyes to behold, throats to sing, mates to love.
>   Life from the sea, warmed by sun, washed by rain.
>   Life from within, giving birth rose to love.
This is the wonder of time; this is the marvel of space;
Out of the stars swung the earth; life upon earth rose to love.

Through a succession of readings this service places death in the larger perspective of Nature's processes. Though grievous, death is part and parcel of the natural order. In the face of death we can still sing of Life. This service is especially appropriate to honor someone who, in life, found peace of mind, inspiration, and wisdom in communion with Nature.

The responsive affirmation can be read by a service leader alone, by a service leader and the congregation together, or responsively by a service leader and another person.

This is the marvel of humanity, rising to see and to know;
Out of your heart, cry wonder: sing that we live.
—Robert Terry Weston, "Out of the Stars"

SINGERS OF LIFE

Today we have come together because _____ has died. This coming together is an instinct, certainly a human instinct, but more universal than just an instinct of our species alone.

There are reports of what might be called badger "funerals," of a badger dragging the body of its mate to an appropriate site, digging a grave, and then with other badgers who have assembled slowly circling the grave and together uttering a low moaning sound—like a dirge.

Others have reported animals protesting the death of one of their own kind. The naturalist Loren Eisley, in an essay "The Judgment of the Birds," told of such an experience that went beyond animals protesting death to seemingly proclaiming life.

Eisley hastened to declare that he did not seek this experience; it happened by chance. He had been traveling over a mountain for half a day. He sat down to rest, his back against a stump. Though he looked out on a small glade, he was hidden from view. It was warm. He was tired. And he soon fell asleep.

A cry awoke him. He looked into the glade—bathed in shafting light that gave the opening the illusion of a cathedral—and on a dead branch protruding into the glade he saw a nestling squirming in the beak of an enormous raven. Eisley wrote:

> The sound that awoke me was the outraged cries of the nestling's parents, who flew helplessly in circles about the clearing. The sleek black monster was indifferent to them. He gulped, whetted his beak on the dead branch a moment, and sat still. Up to that point the little tragedy had followed the usual pattern. But suddenly, out of that area of woodland, a soft sound of complaint began to rise. Into the glade fluttered small birds of half a dozen varieties drawn by the anguished outcries of the tiny parents.

No one dared to attack the raven. But they cried there in some instinctive common misery, the bereaved and the unbereaved. The glade filled with their soft rustling and their cries. They fluttered as though to point their wings at the murderer. There was a dim, intangible ethic he had violated, that they knew. He was a bird of death.

And he, the murderer, the black bird at the heart of life, sat on there, glistening in the common light, formidable, unmoving, unperturbed, untouchable.

The sighing died. It was then I saw the judgment. It was the judgment of life against death. I will never see it again so forcefully presented. I will never hear it again in notes so tragically prolonged. For in the midst of a protest, they forgot the violence. There, in the clearing, the crystal note of a song sparrow lifted hesitantly in the hush. And finally, after painful fluttering, another took the song, and then another, the song passing from one bird to another, doubtfully at first, as though some evil thing were being slowly forgotten. Till suddenly they took heart and sang from many throats joyously together as birds are known to sing. They sang because life is sweet and sunlight beautiful. They sang under the brooding shadow of the raven. In simple truth they had forgotten the raven, for they were the singers of life, and not of death.

Though we are gathered in the shadow of death, and we must protest that one we have known and loved is dead, let us also be singers of life, because weighing life and death, we too conclude that "life is sweet and sunlight beautiful."

"THE COST"

In her poem "The Cost," Dorothy N. Monroe weighed the gains of living against inevitable death, and concluded that "whatever fate demanded in return for life I'd give."

> Death is not too high a price to pay
> for having lived. Mountains never die,
> nor do the seas or rocks or endless sky.
> Through countless centuries of time, they stay

eternal, deathless. Yet they never live!
If choice there were, I would not hesitate
to choose mortality. Whatever Fate
demanded in return for life I'd give,
for, never to have seen the fertile plains
nor heard the winds nor felt the warm sun on sands
beside the salty sea, nor touched the hands
of those I love—without these, all the gains
of timelessness would not be worth one day
of living and of loving; come what may.

HOMEGOING

We don't know for sure what waits beyond this life. But we do know that death is the fate and physical end of all living things. Edwin Way Teal, in his book *The Wilderness of John Muir*, answered the question of "Where?" in a broad and fitting perspective:

> The rugged old Norsemen spoke of death as *Heimgang*—home-going. So the snowflowers go home when they melt and flow to the sea; and the rock-ferns, after unrolling their fronds to the light and beautifying the rocks, roll them up close again in the autumn and blend with the soil. Myriads of rejoicing living creatures—daily, hourly, perhaps every moment—sink into death's arms, dust to dust, spirit to spirit—waited on, watched over, noticed only by their Maker, each arriving at its own Heaven-dealt destiny. All the merry dwellers of the trees and streams, and the myriad swarms of the air, called into life by the sunbeam of a summer morning, go home through death, wings folded perhaps in the last red rays of sunset of the day they were first tried. Trees towering in the sky, braving storms of centuries, flowers turning faces to the light for a single day or hour, having enjoyed their share of life's feast—all alike pass on and away under the law of death and love. Yet all are our [sisters and] brothers and they enjoy life as we do, share Heaven's blessings with us, die and are buried in hallowed ground, come with us out of eternity and return into eternity. 'Our little lives are rounded with a sleep.'

MEDITATION ON LIFE

We will now share a moment of [silent/musical] meditation, that you may reflect upon the meaning of Life and on the particular life of _____. Remember [her/him] as [she/he] lived. Remember how _____'s life touched your life, filled our common world.

EULOGY

(See "The Eulogy," beginning on page 99, for suggestions.)

BEAUTY NEVER DIES

Those who understand and have a clear vision of how a human life (indeed all living things) fits into the scheme of Creation—arching beyond our little planet, farther than our solar system and the myriad stars of our galaxy, to include all the reaches of the cosmos—are comforted and sustained by the dispassionate beauty of Creation that strangely stirs the passions of our hearts. This beauty, for those who see it, never dies. This is why our hearts and our minds respond so well to the following words. These words seem so true when we remember the beauty of _____'s life. The beauty of [her/his] life was and is one with the beauty of Creation—in life and in death.

> Do not stand at my grave and weep—
> I am not there, I do not sleep.
>
> I am a thousand winds that blow.
> I am the diamond glint on snow.
>
> I am the sunlight on ripened grain.
> I am the gentle autumn rain.
>
> When you wake in the morning hush
> I am the swift, uplifting rush
> of quiet birds in circling flight.

I am the soft starlight at night.

Do not stand at my grave
and weep.
I am not there. I do not sleep.
—Anonymous

TREE OF LIFE

Having remembered _____'s life and having considered _____'s life in the scheme of Nature and Creation, we accept the loss, knowing that Life continues—richer for _____'s having lived.

It is a natural miracle, a miracle that repeats. We should always celebrate that the elements of the cosmos—the inanimate, soulless stuff of stars—came together and became the living and loving person who was _____.

That person touched others and shaped our common world. The force of [her/his] personality—the truth and love of [her/his] life—was part of the onward urge of evolving creation. We are, and we are more, because _____ lived. We are glad _____ lived.

We know that death and love are inextricably joined together. For us human beings this reality has transcended the merely biological. Because we are creatures of memory, our love never ends but passes from person to person.

The Tree of Life to which we so often allude is the symbolic Tree of generation following generation, from time into time. And we can proclaim that _____'s name has been written on this Tree of Life forever.

BENEDICTION

Please stand, as you are able, for a benediction to conclude this service.

We take our benediction from William Cullen Bryant's poetic meditation on death, "Thanatopsis." When you are troubled about _____'s death, or when your hurt over your loss is too great, or when the shadow of death casts a pallor over your spirit, remember these words:

Go forth, under the open sky, and list
To Nature's teachings, while from all around—
Earth and her waters, and the depths of air—
Comes a still voice. . . .

Blessings and
Affirmations

ASSURANCES

We give thanks unto God;
For God is the source of all goodness.
God's loving kindness lasts forever,
As does God's faithfulness to all generations.
—Psalm 100:5, adapted

INVOCATION

God of Grace and Tender Mercies, be with us and bless us gathered here.

The curtain of death has fallen between us and one we love. Give us the strength and the wisdom we need for this hour: the strength to face and to endure our enormous loss and the wisdom to rise above our grief and find ample thanksgiving for _____'s life.

God, who gives us life and receives us when our life is over, keep us and comfort us now. Your Goodness is our strength. Your Purpose is our hope. May our confidence in Your Goodness and our faith in Your Purpose be unwavering. And may our words be true to Your Glory and to Your Creation this day and forevermore. Amen.

AFFIRMATION

Death has gathered us here for the end of _____'s life. Let us not just mourn, though mourn we must, for we suffer a great loss. Let us also remem-

This service asks the blessings of a personal God while affirming God's design and purpose, which give us life in birth and take our life in death.

ber the life that _____ lived. And more than remember, let us affirm and celebrate that life as an expression through Life and Love of a Divine Impulse.

Each of us lives between two eternities. Each birth causes us to wonder where the spark of Life comes from. Every death makes us wonder what of that life survives. What we do know is that every human life—with a mind to think and a heart to love—is an expression of the Will to Life—the Spirit of God.

Then in every personality, if we know how to look, we can see ample evidence of Divinity. _____ brought Life and Love into our lives and into our common world. Through _____ we have discovered an aspect of God. This is how we discover God, through and in a life like our own.

Though death claims everyone, there are certain qualities of our lives that will never die, but will live on in this tangible realm between the two eternities of birth and death. So, even in the midst of our grief, let us affirm and celebrate the life of _____ because

> A human life is holy,
>   for it comes from God
>   and it returns to God:
> A human life is holy
>   in its becoming.
> A human life is holy
>   in its living.
> And a human life is holy
>   in its dying.

We Are Gathered

It is good we have come together:

- to mourn _____'s death,
- to remember _____'s personality and life,
- to say "yes" to that which never dies,
- to express our gratitude for God's gifts and graces,
- to invoke the faith that will let us continue living bravely.

PRAYER

This is our special prayer:

May they who knew _____ the best and loved [her/him] the most be comforted by Divine Compassion.

May _____ find comfort in one another. Their sharp and deep grief gives them an empathy beyond all words—an empathy that gives them strength and the assurance that they are not alone.

May they find comfort in the community of women and men who grieve with them, who want to help and offer an ongoing compassion—the compassion of all humanity in every age.

May they find comfort in that which never dies, but lives forever in the bosom of Nature: the whisper of wind, the refreshment of rain, the round embrace of sky, the warm touch of sunlight, the sparkle of light on water—the comfort of those things that seemingly never change and give us glimpses of the Eternal.

"Blessed are they that mourn, for they shall be comforted."

Spirit of Comfort and Love, grant that this may be so for those whose grief is sharp and deep today. Amen.

A DIVINE PROVIDENCE

This we can believe, that a Divine Providence guides the ways of this world, making out of all individual lives a Meaning that is greater than every death—no matter how shattering a death may seem.

This Meaning is not easy to describe, because it has many parts—many smaller meanings. There is the meaning of a human life lived so that it becomes a world itself. There is the meaning of life touching life—of world touching world. There is the meaning of love turned to grief. There is the meaning of grief awakening you to things you have neglected but which now seem so valuable and so worth cultivating. There is the meaning of compassion and empathy—a deeper river to the human condition than you had ever known. There is the meaning of Life cycling and surviving through the generations. There is the meaning of forgiveness—of self, of the deceased, of Life, of God. There is the meaning of acceptance—it is right and fitting that things are so.

These meanings and more come together in a harmony that makes one Meaning in which all things are comprehended and in which there is a Great Peace that rises above all the strains of the Earth. Surely this is the Peace that passes all understanding.

Each of us has the need to find in the midst of this tragedy a meaning or two to suit our own personal needs. Your heart will tell you what your need is. Listen and be open. The meaning will find you. Providence has created us in such a way that what we seek—in integrity and dignity, with humility and sincerity—we shall always, if not immediately, be given.

We are adequate to any challenge with which Providence confronts us, because Providence has provided for us with inner resources and strengths, the comfort and compassion of other women and men.

This is a moment now to be thoughtful and to be self-aware. What do you need and seek now?

This is also a moment to remember _____. How did [her/his] life touch you? What prayer do you offer on _____'s behalf?

[With music/In silence] we enter into a quiet time to search our thoughts and to be in touch with our feelings.

EULOGY

(See "The Eulogy," beginning on page 99, for suggestions.)

BLESSINGS FOR THOSE WHO GRIEVE

Let us remember once again those who mourn _____'s death the most: _____.

May they be granted strength, wisdom, and thanksgiving: strength to bear this loss; wisdom to find meaning and purpose in the design of life; and thanksgiving for a life that touched, but more than touched, that filled our lives and helped create our common world.

May forgiveness and acceptance lead them to a Meaning in which all things are comprehended and in which there is a Great Peace.

We ask this in the name of the God of Love whose Compassion knows no limit.

ADIEU

Though our sorrow is great, we are glad that _____'s life filled our lives and enriched our common world—with thought and word, with love and laughter.

May we never forget _____'s friendly and kindly ways, as well as [her/his] passions and concerns.

May _____ live in Eternity's embrace forever.

It is never easy to say a final goodbye. But now we must. So with heavy heart, but with true joy that _____ lived and loved, we leave [her/him] to the care of God's Eternity.

And as we say good-bye to one we hold dear, be our confidence and our trust, O God of Life and of Death. Amen.

BENEDICTION

Please rise, as you are able, for our benediction.

May we take inspiration from glimmers of the Divine that we see through the lives of our fellow women and men. From this moment on we will live our lives with a surer faith, a greater hope, and a more steadfast love, so that the Spirit of God will move with us and dwell among us. Let this dedication be our living memorial to the life of _____.

And may the peace that passes understanding,
The peace of the Spirit that rises above all the strains of the earth,
Be with us now and forevermore. Amen.

A Meditation
of Candles

MEDITATION

There is a Mysterious Power that animates every living thing, a
Mysterious Power that sustains what we call Life. We do not know where we come
from when we are born. We do not know where we go when we die.
But we do know the life we live between the two eternities of being born and
having to die.
Between these two eternities is our world—our life.
Some of us call the Source of Life, this Mysterious Power, God.
Some of us prefer another name: Eternal Being, or Creative Force, or Spirit of Life,
or perhaps simply, Love.
Some of us do not know what to call this Mysterious Power, for all names seem
somehow inadequate.

Yet we feel this Mysterious Power at the center of our unique beings.
We experience it through the changes of our individual lives.
We see and sense it at work in the life and in the changes of every other living
thing.

Like a flame passing from candle to candle, this Mysterious Power passes from
being to being and from generation to generation.
This Mysterious Power is the Unity of the whole of creation—past, present,
and future.

By lighting candles, a time-honored way of focusing and expressing intentions, a symbolic flame passes from the Mysterious Source of Life to the deceased, and through the deceased's flame to candles representing elements of grief, remembrance, and affirmation. The eulogy for this service uses an optional, though recommended, lighting of candles in which each person attending the service has an opportunity to participate. This service works especially well with smaller settings, but can be used for larger groups as well.

There is a Mysterious Power that animates every living thing, a Mysterious
Power that sustains Life through the unending cycle of the generations.

In honor of this Mysterious Power we light a candle.

CANDLE OF MEMORY

From this candle we light a candle in memory of _____'s life. Let this
flame symbolize all human life as well as Life. It is a fragile flame, and it can be
extinguished by the vagaries of a gust of air—one of the guises of fate. But even
if fate does not end a life unexpectedly, the burning flame will eventually
consume the candle. A candle has its allotted span to burn. (So a human life has
its allotted span of years to live.) Yet while it burns—for a short span or a long
span of time—it radiates light and heat. And flame kindles flame; life begets life.
The glow and heat, the passion of life, are passed on; so long after the candle
is extinguished or consumed, the fire of life and love still burns. A human life
also continues in the lives it has both engendered and influenced.

 Stare at the flame, then look away (or even shut your eyes). As the eye
remembers the light, so the mind remembers a person who has died.

 Though the flame of _____'s life has been extinguished, our
memory's eye still sees the person; and our mind remembers the power of [her/
his] personality—how _____ walked through [her/his] time and world;
how [her/his] life touched us and shaped our lives.

 In remembrance and in honor of _____, we shall light our other
candles in this memorial service from the candle we have lighted for [her/him].

CANDLE OF COMMUNITY

We light this candle to signify the community we create.

 It is good to be together at such a time as this. We need one another in
our grief and in our love. The deep loss of death and the accompanying emotion
of grief are best comforted by our fellow women and men. Friendly faces, kindly
touches, warm embraces, halting words, or no words at all convey shared
empathy.

A variety of candle holders in different heights for 12" tapers and a 5" column candle on a tall base to represent the Mysterious Power of Life make an impressive display. The candle representing the deceased should stand taller than the other tapers. While these candles can be lighted by the service leader alone, having appropriate family and friends to light them creates a positive effect.

We also seek together a meaning in which all things are comprehended. Death has a strange way of sorting out the essentials of life and living, and we see clearly, though through our tears, what really matters. Family and the extended family that includes friends are things that really matter.

It is good, right, and fitting in the face of death that we have come together today:

- to remember the person that _____ was;
- to mourn [her/his] death while celebrating [her/his] life;
- to seek a meaning in which all things are comprehended;
- to find each other to receive comfort and also, as each is able, to give comfort.

CANDLE OF GRIEF

We light this candle to acknowledge those who loved _____ the most and feel [her/his] death most grievously. We especially remember _____.

We cannot pretend to make amends for your loss. But we can give you the continuing promise that we shall walk quietly beside you—hearing your words, seeking to understand the depth of your loss and the pain of your grief, and giving you encouragement and support to continue living.

We pray that you receive the healing gifts of courage, wisdom, and thanksgiving: courage to accept the reality of _____'s death; wisdom that life and death, joy and sorrow are joined; and thanksgiving to celebrate the life that was _____'s life.

CANDLE OF JOY

We light this candle to signify that our sorrow and joy are one.

We cannot deny the grief that death brings. We must let it spill from our hearts. We must let our sorrow have its time, because our joy has had its time. A wise man, James Martineau, wrote:

> We have a human right to our sorrow. To blame the deep grief which bereavement awakens, is to censure all strong human attachment. The more intense the delight in their presence, the more poignant the

impression of their absence; and you cannot destroy the anguish unless you forbid the joy. A morality which rebukes sorrow rebukes love.

William Blake declared, "Joy and woe are woven fine. . . . It is right it should be so, [we were] made for joy and woe."

It is because we knew, loved, and delighted in _____, that we feel such a sorrow for [her/his] death. Our joy came first. Because of the joy, we feel such a sorrow now. Though that sorrow is strong just now, there will be a new day, when once again our joy in _____'s life will be greater than our sorrow in [her/his] absence.

Candle for the Mystery of Life and Death

We light this candle to honor the mystery of Life.

William Shakespeare wrote, "We are such stuff as dreams are made of, and our life is rounded with a sleep." In awe and wonder our thoughts leap from understanding to understanding about a human life and the double mystery of where we come from when we are born and where we go when we die.

This is a time for each of us to find the quiet center and meditate:

- to gather our individual feelings and thoughts,
- to meditate upon the meaning of this occasion,
- to offer a private and final farewell,
- to offer a prayer,
- to remember the person that _____ was and to acknowledge how [she/he] lives on in us.

[With music/In silence] we enter into this time of personal reflection, meditation, and prayer.

Eulogy

(See "The Eulogy," beginning on page 99, or "Personal Remembrances" below.)

PERSONAL REMEMBRANCES

Now is the time for you, if you wish, to come forward and light a candle in memory of _____. After lighting your candle, you may offer your personal tribute—an anecdote, a story, a remembrance.

For these personal remembrances use votive candles or tea lights.

CANDLE OF THANKSGIVING

We light this candle in thanksgiving.

We are thankful for the gifts of Life even though our individual lives are "rounded by a sleep."

We are thankful for _____'s life. We are glad to have seen _____'s face, to have been influenced by _____'s personality and ways, to have loved [her/him] and to have been loved by [her/him] in return.

_____'s deeds continue to influence those [she/he] touched and our larger world, for we are all woven into one tapestry.

We are thankful that time lessens and memories heal the grief we feel at death, bringing ever deeper understandings and a more loving acceptance of [her/him] who has died.

We are thankful for the comfort we give one another, which has grown among us this hour.

We are thankful that Life continues, passing from generation to generation.

We are thankful for the love that never dies. It is true that "Love bears all things, believes all things, hopes all things, endures all things. Love never ends." (Paul, I Corinthians 13:7)

CANDLE OF LOVE

And so we light a final candle for Love:
- the love we have for Life and its Mysterious but Sure Source, which many of us name God;
- the love that _____ had for us;
- the love we have for _____;
- the love that has brought us together.

In the spirit of this love we say our "good-bye" to _____.

CLOSING WORDS AND BENEDICTION

Please rise as you are able so we may stand together as we conclude this service of remembrance and celebration, a service of sorrow and joy for the life of _____.

    We extinguish _____'s candle. But as we do, we see that the candle of Life still burns as do the candles of community, thanksgiving, and love we have lighted from _____'s flame. This is our benediction:

> Spirit of Life be with us
> Giving us the peace of acceptance and understanding
> And the assurance in those things that never die—
> Those things that pass from person to person
>   through the generations into eternity—
> Especially Love.
> In the spirit of Love we have gathered.
> In the spirit of Love we depart.

A Bouquet
of Flowers

WELCOME

It is good to be together. We need each other now to face and understand
_____'s death.

    Our grief is great. But our love is stronger than even our grief:

- our love for _____,
- our love for _____'s family,
- our love for each other,
- our love for all humanity,
- our love for Life.

    Our love compels us to fashion a memorial service of celebration, because we are glad that _____ lived, that [she/he] was with us for _____ years.

    _____ was full of life and gave life to us—richer in things, wiser in thoughts, more abundant in those qualities of [wife/husband, mother/father, sister/brother, friend, coworker] that brought love to our world and made it a better place through [her/his] labors.

    We can never hope to speak to all aspects of _____'s life this [morning/afternoon/evening].

    Our offerings of memory, love, and intention will be like the flowers you hold in your hands. Gathered together they will make a bouquet of beauty. And you will take away with you a flower from that bouquet to signify what _____ gave you and to signify perhaps a new insight or understanding about [her/his] life—how that life filled our common world.

This service draws upon the beauty of flowers and the gathering of a community bouquet. It emphasizes unending love and celebration more than grief. This service works well with a small to mid-size gathering, but can be used for larger gatherings, too.

    People receive a stemmed flower as they enter the room. If the gathering is relatively small, the chairs can be arranged in a semi-circle with an appropriate table for the vase(s) as a focal point. For larger gatherings and a more conventional arrangement of chairs, arrange an altar-like table with a vase(s) at center-front.

A QUIET MOMENT

Now we will share a quiet moment so that each of us might:
- remember the person _____was,
- how _____ touched us personally and lives in us forever;
- and how _____ contributed to making each of us the person we are.

Be in touch with your feelings, whatever those feelings might be. Do not be afraid where they might take you, because together we can face whatever we must face.

Say your heartfelt good-bye, your adieu to _____.

This is a time to reflect, to meditate, and perhaps offer your simple prayer.

[With music/In silence] we enter this quiet moment.

A BOUQUET OF MEMORIES

Now we will make a bouquet out of our memories and love for _____.

Please come forward and place your flower in the vase. If you wish and are able, you may offer us your remembrance of _____, or you may offer your reflections on the meaning of this occasion.

We know and respect that you may not be able or may not want to say anything at this time. (Indeed, silence sometimes shows more than words can express.) You may simply, in silence, place your flower in the vase as your tribute to the memory of _____ and in honor of the weaving of relationships that has gathered us together.

ANOTHER QUIET MOMENT

This bouquet of flowers symbolizes _____'s life. That life was abundant and beautiful. [She/he] touched many people in more ways than we can ever describe.

This bouquet also symbolizes the weaving of our lives into a community through _____'s living and loving.

As we enter into another quiet moment [of music/of silence], contemplate the meanings of this symbolic bouquet.

AN ACCOUNTING

We are glad _____ lived.

[Her/his] life filled our lives and helped create our common world, making it a better place to live and love.

We will remember [her/him] each in our private way forever.

And we will not forget how _____'s life gathers us into a bouquet of humanity—a blessed community.

We will be there for one another when we are needed to comfort, to guide, and to help as we are able.

Together we will survive the grief we feel and once again live—more deeply and more abundantly because _____ lived.

Though we can never replace _____ in the days of our lives, [she/he] remains an immortal presence in us, because Love never ends.

BENEDICTION

In the spirit of Love we close this celebration of the life of _____.

Let us go in peace and live together in charity, taking from and giving to one another—as we need and as we are able—the gifts of courage, wisdom, and thanksgiving.

A FLOWER IN REMEMBRANCE

As a symbol of _____'s influence on us and of our unending Love for _____, please take a flower from the vase as you depart.

Golden Silence

Death Gathers Us

Today we face one of Life's most difficult moments. We suffer a loss—the death of _____.

It's good to be together. More than anything else we need one another right now. Each of us grieves. And when we grieve together, the healing begins.

Just by being here each of us gives comfort to everyone else. If only for this hour we are joined in a compassionate family. Yes, it's good to be together.

At a time like this words frequently fall short of what we really want to say. Yet we find ourselves trying to express not just our grief, but also our joyful feelings for _____. We will recall our love for [her/him] and we will recall [her/his] love for us. And we also want to remember _____ as [she/he] was—when we saw [her/his] face and knew [her/his] touch and heard [her/him] speak.

Our words are like our tears, welling in our eyes until they are too full. Then they must stream and fall.

A Listening Silence

Our service to honor _____'s memory and to express our tumultuous emotions and our avalanche of thoughts will be shaped by what is called a "listening silence." We will now try out this "listening silence."

Alone—each in her or his private chamber of thoughts, yet aware of the presence of one another—we share a period of silence. In this silence:

This service reflects the Quaker (Society of Friends) tradition of the silent service and has a deep and still serenity. It anticipates the days to come. And while it does verbalize a few thoughts and feelings that death brings, it asserts that certain emotions and thoughts are beyond words.

listen . . .

    . . . to hear what lies in your mind and in your heart;

listen . . .

    . . . to hear a still, small voice;

listen . . .

    . . . to hear the Infinite's assurances and timeless wisdom.

A "listening silence" can often show more concern than any spilling rush of words.

First Silence

Letting the Spirit Speak

Let us now remember _____—the person who lived and whose life touched ours. We shall follow the Quaker custom of letting the spirit speak to us in the midst of collective quiet.

Maybe the Spirit of Life will speak through you with a wonderful wisdom about living and dying.

Maybe the spirit of _____'s life will come into your consciousness, and you will share an impression, memory, or anecdote about [her/him].

Maybe the spirit of a fellow mourner—present or absent—will touch you, and you will offer words of condolence and comfort.

As before, *listen* and *hear*. If what you hear in your mind is compelling, speak aloud and share the spirit that is speaking within you, though your words may seem inadequate or halting. This is what we mean by "letting the spirit move you."

Second Silence and Personal Offerings

The Great Peace

As your grief follows its course, there will be many times in the days to come when silence will happen without your actively seeking it. Or an instinct will lead you into a more deliberate quiet time. In either instance, you will find what is expressed in the following meditation, "The Great Peace" by Robert Terry Weston:

Speaker sits down, monitoring a silence of five minutes. A musical selection appropriately reflective and lasting about two or three minutes—brings the group back to words.

Two or three people can be primed in advance to speak, setting an example. The service leader must monitor the pace of this silence so that there is ample oppor-tunity for all who wish to speak. When the service leader feels that enough time has been allowed, the service can proceed with "The Great Peace."

Always there is something,
Something that lives on when folly has burned itself out;
When the leaves are sere, and fall, one by one;
When the hair is white,
And the hands tremble,
And cannot quite find what they seek;
Always there is something.
Perhaps it is a whisper in the night,
Or a great silence, when the planes are gone,
And the cars are silent beside the highways,
And the children are asleep,
And the heart can hear a soundless voice.
Always there is something, something beyond all time.
The past that has hurt slips away:
The humiliations, the failures, the resentment,
The sorrows, the haunting fears, dissolve into the healing night.
The darkness is no longer darkness, but a comforting presence,
And it comes, a great peace, flooding the heart.
It comes, a sense of healing forgiveness,
A sense of comprehending and forgiving compassion,
A meaning in which all things are comprehended and made whole
Though we, accepting, comprehend it not.
Always there is something, and we, knowing this, need never fear
     again,
Nor hate, nor grieve, for there is always something
Above defeat and success alike,
And to know and feel this
Is to know the great peace.

Be assured that whatever you feel, however great your grief over
_____'s death might be, and however terrible or conflicting your emotions might be right now, be assured that memories will heal and time will lessen your hurt. The Great Peace awaits, too.

You can trust in these things working. Be expectant, but don't be demanding. In the days ahead let yourself be quiet. In the silence—if you *listen*—

what you need to endure and to live again will be whispered to you out of the quiet.

Affirmation

We are glad _____ lived—that [her/his] life touched our lives and many others. We are all connected and our strength is the strength of many. Though death has severed the physical cord, our memories and love for _____ are strong. And in [her/his] death the strong cords of grief and compassion join us together in new and strong ways of interdependence. In _____'s death we have found one another. In death the Web of Life is never weakened but made even stronger.

_____ is with us in our minds and in our hearts forever.

Leaving in Silence

We have shaped our service in honor of _____ with silence—inviting the Spirit of Life and Love to speak to us and through us.

Let us leave this service in silence, even as we leave _____ to the Silence of Eternity.

DRAWING THE CIRCLE

Come into this circle of loss.
Come into this circle of compassion.
Come into this circle of memory.
Come into this circle of Love.

We mourn the death of _____, who is no longer with us in the flesh. But [her/his] spirit dwells in our minds, hearts, and in the way [her/his] deeds shaped our common world.

Our loss, the hurt we feel, our reaching out to one another do not close the circle, but open it to all our sisters and brothers. We are gathered into the sacred circle of all humanity, through the one fate that shapes our lives and through the grief that death always brings.

INVOCATION

Creator, You have given us life—a circle of days. And You have made it so that generation follows generation, so that Life endures—circle repeating circle. This is how You give Life and keep Life. And You have put death at the end of our days, closing the circle of each life.

We know this. But still death brings us deep loss, and we mourn our loss. So we seek to understand and accept as we are able, that living is losing those we love and eventually dying ourselves.

Native American spirituality has a contemporary appeal. This service adapts the "medicine wheel" concept of Native American spirituality, asking for inspiration and counsel of the traditional four directions (and the animal spirits associated with those directions). The ritual of drumming can be used to pace and accentuate this service.

Creator, take us beyond grief to acceptance and understanding. Make our steps strong and steady so that we shall travel the healing circle—from loss and grief to living and joy once again.

Creator, take us now around the sacred circle of the four directions. Take us first to Illumination (where the eagle soars)—that we might see clearly. Next take us to Innocence (the vision of the mouse)—that we may grieve deeply and trust simply. Then take us to Introspection (the cave of the bear)—that we may look into our individual being, knowing what lies in the secret chambers of our mind and heart. And finally take us to Wisdom (the spirit of the buffalo)—that we may come to that peace that passes understanding.

BLESSING OF ILLUMINATION

O Creator, give us a broad vision clear of distorting and clouding emotions. Let us be like an eagle soaring in the clear yellow light of the sun.

Let us see in our memory's eye _____ as [she/he] lived. [She/he] was one sort of person and [her/his] personality touched many in a variety of ways. Give us the vision that sees the span of _____'s years on the earth.

Let us see the way that death fits into Life—that living is also dying. _____'s life belonged to the way of all living things.

Our sense of loss—the emotional pain we feel—results from the joy and delight we had in _____'s life. Let us see that our sorrow and joy are one. Let us be glad for _____'s personality and for the way [she/he] lived [her/his] life.

BLESSING OF INNOCENCE

O Creator, give us the innocence to mourn—to be passionate and true to our feelings. Let us be like a humble mouse close to the green earth.

Death is a grievous event. We feel the void left by _____'s dying. We are filled with dread. Let us not be afraid of our feelings, but trusting that we can endure even the emptiest depths of our grief. We are able, and we also have the strength of our family and friends who are with us in the sacred circle.

Let us be open and even vulnerable before one another. This is not a time for false displays. No one among us is invulnerable or indifferent. We can reach out to one another to comfort, and we can be comforted if we can be humble in the face of _____'s death.

No one person has the answers to the questions that tumble at this time. Why? Could anything have been done? What comes after death? What are these troubling emotions that are swirling? Yet together, in humility and honesty, we can find the answers that spiral through the circle of our common humanity.

BLESSING OF INTROSPECTION

O Creator, take each of us into the sacred circle of Self—that each might reflect upon the meaning of this occasion. Let us be like a bear that has retreated into the darkness of the cave.

Take each of us into our private memories of how _____'s life touched and filled our individual lives.

Take each of us beyond our own memories into somewhere even more private, where each of us encounters our own mortality. Let a sense of empathy and understanding open us up to Life—that we shall from this moment on not waste our days. Let this sense open us up to one another, too, in our wanting and in our giving.

[Silence/Music] takes us into a time for personal reflection so that we may go deeply into our individual being:

- to remember,
- to offer a prayer for _____,
- to think about the meaning of this moment,
- to see our own life in perspective.

EULOGY

(See "The Eulogy," beginning on page 99, for suggestions.)

BLESSING OF WISDOM

O Creator, take us now to wisdom—that our understanding of _____'s death and our thanksgiving for _____'s life will lead us to acceptance and a peace that passes understanding. (Let us be like a sacred white buffalo who understands and accepts.)

We accept what we cannot change. And though in our heart we may have raged against _____'s death, we must now accept the reality.

And our gratitude—our joy and delight—is real: that we knew [her/him]; that [she/he] knew us; that our memories of _____ will last forever; and that those memories will help us heal our grief.

Though our understanding has its limits, where our understanding ends, a strange and wonderful peace begins—a peace we can only say has its source in You and Your Creation.

We are not separated but bound to you, O Creator—one with You in our Life and in our Death.

CLOSING THE CIRCLE

To close the circle, let us listen to a poem by Wendell Berry:

> Within the circle of our lives
> we dance the circle of the years,
> the circles of the seasons
> within the circles of the years,
> the cycles of the moon
> within the circles of the seasons,
> the circles of our reasons
> within the cycles of the moon.
>
> Again, again we come and go,
> changed, changing. Hands
> join, unjoin in love and fear,
> grief and joy. The circles turn,
> each giving into each, into all.
> Only music keeps us here,
>
> each by all the others held.
> In the hold of hands and eyes

we turn in pairs, that joining
joining each to all again.

And then we turn aside, alone,
out of the sunlight gone

into the darker circles of return.
                    —"Song(4)"

A Quilt of
Memories
and Love

INTENTIONS

Our sister _____ is dead. In gathering pieces of fabric and stitching them into a single cloth—a quilt—we are piecing together our memories, our feelings, our wisdom as we face this difficult death. May the quilt we make be a beautifully patterned comforter for our grief this day and in the days to come.

AFFIRMATIONS

(These affirmations can be particularly effective if each one beginning with "It is" is spoken by a different voice.)

It is good to be together now. We need one another. Now we look at friendly faces and touch in the most ancient of all languages, conveying the deepest feelings beyond all words.

It is good to cry because our hearts are torn. We feel the heartache of others as well as we feel our own heartache.

It is good to remember with smiles and laughter, as well as with tears, the person _____ was, how she filled our world and brightened our days. Healing the hurt begins with remembering. Our memories of _____ can never be taken from us, nor shall we ever forget.

It is good to let our sorrows and our memories reach out beyond this death, beyond this hour to include others whom death has taken from our lives. This death awakens deeper memories.

This is a service for women. It uses the tradition of quilt making to symbolize both the deceased's life and the sisterhood of the gathered women. (This service can be adapted for a gathering of women and men.) This service works well as a supplementary memorial service after a public memorial service.

Those who will be attending can be encouraged in advance to bring a quilt square or a special piece of fabric to contribute to the symbolic quilt fashioned at the heart of this service.

Those organizing the service should give special attention to the setup. Arrange the chairs in a circle around a low table. A large white cloth, a basket of additional fabric squares, a box of pins, and a candle in a holder complete the special preparations.

Slowly read this meditation to let imaginations participate fully.

It is good to be joined with all who have ever known death and have grieved. A wise woman, Helen Keller, once explained this with these words:

> We bereaved are not alone. We belong to the largest company in all the world—the company who has known suffering. When it seems that our sorrow is too great to be borne, let us think of the great family of the heavy-hearted into which our grief has given us entrance, and inevitably we will feel about us then, their arms, their sympathy, their understanding.
>
> —from *We Bereaved*

CENTERING AND GATHERING

Now close your eyes.

Know what you bring and what we create together this [morning/afternoon/evening].

Acknowledge your loss—what is gone from your life because _____ is dead.

Feel your grief. Do not hold back your tears. They are the rain of your friendship, the salt of your love.

Gently hold your compassion, your heartache to comfort and to share the grief of those who suffer the loss of _____ the most. Be especially mindful of those whose grief is deepest.

Now let your memories of _____ rise from the depths of your mind.

Say a heartfelt thank you that _____ lived—that she touched you and her life filled your life with her spirit and her deeds. Say a private thank you that her life filled our world and made it a better place.

Remember her kindly ways, how she walked and talked with you. Remember her face. Remember her embrace and the touch of her hands.

With eyes still closed, reach out to hold the hands of the sisters sitting next to you. Each of us has suffered a loss. Each of us grieves. Each of us reaches out to give comfort and to be comforted in turn. Each of us remembers the woman _____ was.

Each of us is a piece of a quilt—a quilt of loss and grief, of memory and love. Our fingers are like stitches, binding a single fabric from our many pieces.

A Favorite Song

"_____" was a favorite song of _____'s. You may, if you want, sing or hum along while the music plays.

As the music plays, a basket of quilt pieces will be passed around the circle. When the basket comes to you, choose a piece, if you have not brought a square with you, on which to focus your memories of and love for _____.

Quilting Memories and Love

Now, one at a time, pin your quilt piece to the white cloth. While securing your piece of cloth, you may, if you wish, offer your personal tribute to _____, telling how her life touched you and how you especially remember her now. If you prefer, you may just pin your piece to the other pieces as a silent tribute.

Notice how the various pieces fit into one another to form a pattern, a pattern that is repeated in the pattern of your remembrances. _____ was certainly a unique, vital woman.

A service leader unfolds a large white cloth and drapes it like a tablecloth over a low table in the center of the group. A box of straight pins is handy.

Meditation on Death

On the quilt of memories and love, a quilt reminding us of _____ and giving us a wonderful comfort, we place this candle in the center of the quilt and light it to consecrate these thoughts.

What can we say about death? It is a mystery, and we do not know what happens to a person when they die. It is a part of life and no one can escape it. It makes us humble and leads us into Life.

We have the strength to face it, because we must. We are adequate for all that Life presents us.

We have the strength to face this death, because we have the support of our family and friends. Our strength is the strength of many.

We shall survive this death, no matter how keen and deep our grief, and eventually live again. And we shall live more lovingly than we lived before.

George Eliot, in her "Letters," explored the meaning and ways of death in writing:

> For the first sharp pangs there is no comfort; whatever goodness may surround us, darkness and silence hang about our pain. But slowly, the clinging companionship with the dead is linked with our living affections and duties, and we begin to feel our sorrow as a solemn initiation, preparing us for that sense of loving, pitying fellowship with the fullest human lot, which, I think, no one who has tasted it will deny it to be the chief blessedness of our life. And especially to know what the last parting is, seems needful to give the utmost sanctity of tenderness to our relations with each other.

Though death extinguishes a life, it paradoxically can lead us—like a light—into a deeper reality. As we leave this room, let us leave more tenderly joined to one another and to Life than when we came in. This is _____'s final gift: In her death we have found one another.

BENEDICTION

Please stand together and hold hands one final time.

> Out of her Mother she came,
> —born as we all are born.
> And she returns to the Mother
> —who eventually embraces us all—
> To dissolve in the earth
> And be with Her forever and forever.

The service leader extinguishes the candle.

EXTINGUISHING THE CANDLE

As we extinguish the candle signifying the mystery of death, in quietness of spirit embrace and greet one another.

(The pinned pieces can be later sewn and made into an actual quilt to present to a family member of the deceased.)

Gathered by Love: A Service for the Loss of an Infant

Who can say when love begins? Love is eternal—a continuity. What or whom we love, we have loved before our meeting. It was our heart's desire first.

And when our love finds its object—takes form and becomes real—our hearts swell so much, we can't find words to adequately express what we are experiencing.

We are gathered now by a love that became real—so real that hearts overflowed again and again and again, while love was taking form in a mother's womb.

Our hopes were so great. Our dreams so vivid. We waited and planned. Our lives were changing. And now we confront a tragic loss and face a mountain of grief. It's immense, because our love was so simple and so pure—as simple and pure as the child of our hopes and dreams.

Nothing about our loss seems right. Nothing!

Nothing can make it right. Nothing!

Instead we seek—yes, pray—for tender mercies:

- for understanding that will eventually bring us a measure of peace;
- for forgiveness for that which makes us feel ashamed and guilty, and also forgiveness for a cruel Fate that allowed this tragedy to happen;
- for memory that will assure that this love "born out of time" will not be forgotten;
- for compassion, that we will not be alone at such a difficult time;
- for companionship, that family and friends will be there to hear, to hold, to help us begin to heal;

Broadly constructed so as to be adaptable to address miscarriage, stillbirth, and early infant death, this service acknowledges a unique grief. Because it is so easily misunderstood, except by those who have experienced it, perinatal or neonatal bereavement demands special attention. Such a service can be particularly therapeutic, even years after the event. This service focuses on the mother's unique loss, then the father's or partner's grief. It is sensitive in including others touched by concentric circles of grief. If the mother is single, exclude those parts that speak to a partner.

- for acceptance that what we can't change must not only be endured but will paradoxically give us more abundant life in time.

AN ACCOUNTING OF GRIEF

This special grief is like a pebble dropped in water—concentric circles radiating from the mother and the [father/partner] to include siblings, grandparents, and other relatives, friends, co-workers, colleagues, and even the health team and caregivers.

In particular we honor the grief of the parents, _____ and _____.

The mother bears the most profound grief of all—a grief as intimate and as private as her own body. She may feel as though she has lost her mind. She's so empty, so utterly alone. It seems she can't possibly go on. "Will I ever get over it?" she wonders, even as she asks a persistent, unanswerable question, "Why?" And frustration becomes anger, an objectless anger that she may turn inward.

She may feel that the loss is somehow her fault. She torments herself with ifs: if only she hadn't done that, or if only she had done this, the love growing in her might have lived.

The special room with its special things readied for the child she anticipated may be too painfully evocative to enter. A shelf of baby food or stacked cartons of diapers in a grocery store may pierce her with a sharp grief that catches her breath. Every pregnant woman may remind her of her own intense love, and she feels jealousy and resentment. Such thoughts may fill her with shame and guilt, no matter how reasonable her feelings are.

Perhaps the intensity of her grief makes her think she's demanding too much from her spouse, her family, or her friends; or that she's neglecting those who need her. But how can she even think of giving when her own needs are so intense?

The [father/partner] grieves too, and differently. Every instinct makes [him/her] want to make right what cannot be made right. Fantasy may plague [him/her], too. "What could I have done differently?" This fantasy can become blame, as well as make [him/her] feel inadequate.

[He/she] has been cheated. [He/she] knows what the poet Ben Jonson lamented at the loss of his first son:

"Farewell, thou Child of my right hand and joy!
My sinne [sic] was too much hope of thee. . . ."

The partners may feel a strange and troubling ambivalence between them: They share a grief. Yet that grief is particular. Each is strangely alone with a unique experience of love lost.

Be assured that while you may feel alone, each in your own way as well as alone together, others have suffered as you suffer. Others will follow you. You are forever changed, deeply saddened but also made wiser. You belong to a compassionate community unlike any other. Let this silent, comprehending community, the multitude that has shared this unique grief, embrace you.

You who grieve, take comfort and find courage that love never ends. Though you have suffered a terrible loss, one that we can't begin to measure, you have within you forever a love that grew more real day by day by day. All that is beautiful, good, and true will not let it end. You will not let it end, you in whom love has formed and ached to live.

Add additional acknowledgments of others who are affected by this loss: sibling children, grandparents, aunts and uncles, close friends, caregivers.

Music, Silent Reflection, and Placing Objects in a Memory Box

Select a piece of music, such as Ravel's haunting and beautiful "Pavane for a Dying Princess." Following the selection, personal condolences might be spoken aloud or expressed silently by lighting votive candles. Following the lead of those who have also lost an infant, you might find it meaningful to create a "memory box" in which you lovingly place keepsakes, such as sonograms, receiving blankets, cards and letters of condolence.

Affirmation

My Little One, My Dear One, My Love

My little one, my dear one, my love,
You will be with me forever:
in the thin sunlight and long shadows
of a clear winter's day;
in the dawn excitement of birds

sounding in early spring;
in the rustle of heavy-leafed trees
in a mid-summer's night;
in the rich aromas and bright colors
of a warm autumn day.
All that is excellent,
brushed by Life's
brightness and shadow,
will remind me of you,
My little one, my dear one, my love.
You will beat with my heart,
see through my eyes,
hear with my ears,
feel on my skin.
Because your soul is mingled with my soul,
forever,
My little one, my dear one, my love.

A Pledge

At this occasion, whatever words we say seem inadequate. You who suffer this loss the most, especially the parents,_____ and _____, are experiencing the deepest grief imaginable.

It is our pledge, our solemn promise, to listen and to try to understand. We know we can't make right what is so wrong. We weep with you. We offer whatever support you may need. When you need to be alone we will respect that need. We'll seek quiet and steady ways, knowing this may be a lingering grief, with each anniversary and holiday bringing your love and its grief to the surface of your soul. Knowing you won't forget, we will remember too, quietly by your side.

In the Spirit of Love, we pray once more for those tender mercies that will help us all to continue—tender mercies for you, who suffer this tragic loss.

BENEDICTION

We affirm:
Love believes all things, hopes all things, endures all things . . .
Love never ends. . . .
Faith, hope, love abide . . .
But the greatest of these is love.

Love has gathered us
And love lets us depart
With renewed faith and hope.

My little one, my dear one, my love,
I release a balloon to the heavens.
Letting go, I lift my love to you.
My eyes follow my love rising into eternity.
Bless you, my little one, my dear one, my love.

Mothers who have endured a perinatal or neonatal loss have devised a simple, yet compelling ritual that signifies what cannot be put solely into words: the releasing of a helium balloon, often with a note attached, at the funeral/memorial service or at a subsequent significant anniversary. You might use this ritual to conclude this service.

A Hard Word to Say: A Service Supplement for Suicide

We don't ever totally understand an act such as this—this taking of one's own life. Suicide is a hard word to say. But we must say it, so that in time we can accept it. And even in the midst of our grief we can respect it as a choice—some say the ultimate choice of self-determination. This respect doesn't come easily but it can break upon us like sunlight shafting through a troubled sky. Let it be so now.

We torture ourselves by going over and over again the chain of events leading up to the taking of this life. We wonder, were we attentive enough? Were messages being given? Were there cries for help we didn't hear? Could we have intervened?

Frustration is real. Every fiber of our bodies is poised to fight or run; but there are only shadows with which to contend, and there is nowhere to flee.

We feel anger, too—especially the anger of abandonment. This is the fate of those left behind, who must seek to understand and incorporate such a tragic loss into their living. Our mourning will be troubled and conflicted; we know because it already is.

These and similar emotions reveal that our grief looks to our own lives and our living: the shock, the denial, the anger, the acceptance, and the long journey of recovery and reconstruction that face us.

Yet in the midst of such a complex grief and with so many unanswerable questions, we acknowledge that _____ made [her/his] choice about when and how [she/he] died.

Perhaps _____ felt what Emily Dickinson once expressed: "Tis not that Dying hurts us so—Tis living—hurts us more."

When a death occurs by suicide, the survivors' complex grief is compounded by embarrassment, guilt, and shame. This supplement is intended to be added to the various services just before the silent or musical meditation that precedes the eulogy. This passage acknowledges conflicted feelings of the survivors and places the suicide in the larger context of the whole life of the deceased.

And Emily Dickinson's words are true for us survivors, too. The death has happened. We can deal with that immediately. It will be the living from here on, the long days and the longer nights, that will test us more.

We can't relinquish our grief totally, but let's put it aside as best as we can, if only briefly. Let us be mindful of our companion _____, whose death faces us now—a unique personality to be remembered for all [her/his] years and not just [her/his] final choice. A person is not just one moment or even a few moments, rather the sum of all moments. Let us not objectify _____ by remembering [her/him] only for the choice [she/he] made to end [her/his] life. Let us strive to remember [her/him] as the whole person who lived.

Bless us all with such a wide and open-eyed vision, as we enter a time of quiet remembrance.

A Time to Die: A Service Supplement for Passive Euthanasia

Love isn't easy. It was never meant to be. Love is responsibility. Love is honoring your beloved's wishes. Eventually love is letting go. And sometimes, as with this death, love is helping your beloved to let go too. It was _____'s time; [her/his] body was worn out. All the medicine in the world, all the machines of the healing arts, weren't going to make [her/him] better.

_____ entrusted us with a decision. We accepted that decision reluctantly perhaps, but with respect for _____ and with faith, knowing that while love isn't easy, love gives us courage.

Our acts spoke our unspoken thoughts. It was _____'s time to die. So we said, "Go with our love. Let the suffering and the struggle end. Let peace settle upon your spirit. It is time: not our time, but your time. You have persevered and fought the good fight. Now go gently—yes, gently—into that good night. You deserve, have earned, this final grace. Love and love's companion, compassion, decree it."

It is my hope, yes, my prayer, that those entrusted by _____'s love, to ensure that [her/his] dying would be dignified, that it would not be artificially or unnecessarily prolonged by extraordinary measures, may feel the blessings of that love upon them now. There may be no greater love a person can bestow upon another person than this tenderest of mercies that brings blessed release and eternal peace.

I pray for you tender mercies and an abiding peace that knows you acted from respect and love as you honored that most difficult decision—that it was a time to die.

When death comes to the ill or aged, when there have been indignities and suffering, those who have been given legal power of health care may have made a difficult decision not to extend life by artificial or extraordinary means. Such decisions, acts of passive euthanasia, lay special burdens on those given the responsibility to make them. This supplement, to be used in the various services, reasons that the decision was grounded in a compassionate love. Add it to the consolations for those who grieve, which follows the eulogy.

Go Forth, Under the Open Sky

When thoughts
Of the last bitter hour come like a blight
Over thy spirit, and sad images
Of the stern agony, and shroud, and pall,
And breathless darkness, and the narrow house,
Make thee shudder, and grow sick at heart;—
Go forth, under the open sky, and list
To Nature's teachings, while from all around—
Earth and her waters, and the depths of air—
Comes a still voice. . . .
                —William Cullen Bryant, "Thanatopsis"

Because this is a graveside service, it is more concrete than the other services. This is a powerful service used by itself or in conjunction with the other services. It blends a few traditional sayings from the Judeo-Christian tradition with images of Nature.

Intentions and Feelings

It is good to be together at this time and place, because we need not only the blessings of Nature, but the blessing we can give one another: human concern and support, human comfort, and love. We have been gathered here today by death. But it is not death really, but Life, that has gathered us here—the life that was _____'s and the Life we share. It is because _____ loved us and we loved [her/him] that we honor [her/his] memory with words of intention and feeling by placing [her/his body, the ashes of her/his body] in the Earth.

In an immediate and very real way, because this is such a final and physical act, this is the most difficult one we must do when someone whom we respected and loved has died.

At this time in particular, we feel the cold reality of human mortality. Such feelings and the sentiments they evoke are described by Edna St. Vincent Millay in her poem, "Dirge Without Music."

> I am not resigned to the shutting away of loving hearts in the
>   hard ground.
> So it is, and so it will be, for so it has been, time out of mind:
> Into the darkness they go, the wise and the lovely. Crowned
> With lilies and with laurel they go; but I am not resigned.
>
> Lovers and thinkers, into the earth with you.
> Be one with the dull, the indiscriminate dust.
> A fragment of what you felt, of what you knew,
> A formula, a phrase remains,—but the best is lost.
> . . . .
> Down, down, down into the darkness of the grave
> Gently they go, the beautiful, the tender, the kind;
> Quietly they go, the intelligent, the witty, the brave.
> I know. But I do not approve. And I am not resigned.

Yet now as we stand under the rounding dome of the sky, with the resilient and good Earth beneath our feet, washed by sunlight and air, we intuit things timeless and reassuring.

We know, deep in our flesh, the sure cycles of nature, the fit of a human life span into the seasons of the generations, the Earth, and the Universe: a sublime design. And there is an unmistakable rightness to what we now do, no matter how much we protest this death.

From dust to dust; from spirit to spirit; from eternity to eternity: Between these spans, a human life fits.

At this occasion we remember what _____ was before birth and what [she/he] is after death as well as who [she/he] was in life.

In this setting we know that we are one with Nature and Nature's unchangeable laws. This wonderful holiness uplifts us.

MOMENT OF SILENCE

In humility and awe, before death and Nature, we stand (as we are able) in silence to show our respect and our love for _____.

REMEMBRANCES

This is a time for anyone who wishes to say a few words in memory of _____ to do so.

COMMITTAL

In committing [the body/the remains] of _____ to the hallowed ground of Earth and to the keeping of Eternity, we do so with deep reverence for the body as a creation of the Divine—a unique expression of an Eternal and Abiding, though Mysterious, Love.

Under the round dome of Eternity the earthly remains of _____ shall rest in peace. This grave is consecrated by our memories of and our love for [her/him], but even more by the person [she/he] was and the life [she/he] lived.

Spirit of Life and Love, Eternal God, the spirit of _____ that filled our world with love and delight has become one with your Eternity. Grant to us who grieve this death forgiveness, a sense of comprehending compassion, and a meaning in which all things are understood and made whole. May the love in our hearts join us together in richer ways than before and, in time, lead us to the peace that passes understanding. We know that _____'s spirit will always be with us—[her/his] love for us and our love for [her/him] will never die.

Casket or urn is lowered into ground.

ANCIENT WISDOM

Now we remember these timeless words:

> For everything there is a season and a time for every matter under
> heaven:
> a time to be born, and a time to die; . . .
> a time to seek, and a time to lose; . . .
>
> —Ecclesiastes 3:1-6

A FINAL FAREWELL

We are glad _____ lived. We cherish [her/his] memory.

We leave our dead to the keeping of this peaceful and consecrated plot of earth. With respect we say farewell to _____. In love we will remember [her/him] forever.

Thinking of _____ in this manner, let us all go in quietness of spirit and live in charity with one another.

BENEDICTION

> The courage of the early morning's dawning,
> The strength of the eternal hills,
> The peace of the evening's ending
> And the love of Life
> Be in our hearts.

It had been Bill's wish that his body be cremated after his death, and his ashes be scattered or buried on the property. Kent, Kim, Scott, and I conferred on how we would deal with this request and decided that the entire family would go outside and be party to the ceremony. We agreed to select four different locations on the property that had special significance for Bill, and we would do appropriate readings at each site.

First, we went to the front bank where Bill had so eagerly planted sumac and trailing honeysuckle to keep the earth from eroding. After Kent read the well-known "time" passage from Ecclesiastes, Kent, Scott, Adam, Nick, and I each took up a small scoop of ashes and scattered them. We repeated this ritual three times more in selected locations. Scott read a passage from a poem, and again, we scooped more of the ashes and dropped them at the site of a walnut tree that Bill had planted and nourished so lovingly. Next, we all walked over to the place that had served as the "flower bed" with the peonies, phlox, day lilies, and mock orange bushes Bill and I had planted so many years ago. I did a reading, and we repeated the ritual of the ashes. The last of the ashes were scattered in the wind to the north, at the back of the lot after Kim read a favorite Ogden Nash poem for Bill. We felt Bill was with us. His love and spirit permeated throughout our heartfelt and solemn sacrament.

As we concluded our sober observance, Adam suggested that we sing "Happy Birthday" to Grandpa. Choked with emotion, and with moist eyes and dry throats, we all sang "Happy Birthday" to Bill as lustily as we could, and closed with "we're glad he was born."

The scattering of ashes is such a visceral act that the family often prefers it to be private and informal. The following account of how one family dealt with this solemn and sacred act provides a good example. It was written by Sylvia Savage of Lemont, Illinois, wife of the deceased Bill Savage. Kim, Scott, and Kent are their adult children. Benjamin, Adam, and Nick are grandchildren. Martha and Mary are daughters-in-law.

Since it was so foreign to their more traditional backgrounds, the ceremony was somewhat difficult for Bill's sister, Betty, and for Martha, Mary, and Benjamin, too. They were, however, able to sense the depths of love, caring, emotion, and respect.

More Than Ashes: A Reading for the Interment of Ashes

The fire has consumed
all that is to be consumed.

Left are ashes
and a fragment or two
of heat-tempered bone.

This is not the woman
who was.

Because she was more
than ashes and fragments,
We honor these remains.

What she was—
wife and mother,
worker and friend,
lover and doer—
Compels us to preserve
her memory.

By burying [scattering] these ashes and fragments
and speaking words
of memory and affirmation,

When cremated remains are removed from their container and mixed with the earth, either in burial or scattering, there is something visceral and possibly shocking about the ashes and fragments of bone. Is this all there is at the end of a life? This poetic meditation to be used at such an occasion speaks to counter thoughts and emotions—that the spirit endures, if only in memory. It is easily adapted to apply to a man.

We give our breath
to what was
And has dissolved
into eternity
forever,
But will not be forgotten.

She was
a woman
Who lived and loved
and gave us life.

And we will not forget.

We mingle her ashes and fragments of bone
with Nature
Where her memories are mingled
with Life itself,
Forever.

The Eulogy

The eulogy is the focal point of a funeral or memorial service. It paints a picture of the person who has died, and makes the service personal by stimulating the memories of the mourners. It should honestly remember and affirm the deceased, thereby giving value and honor to her or his character—how the deceased lived life, touched others, and left an indelible mark on our common world.

You can approach the task of presenting a eulogy in several ways.

1. You can elicit spontaneous personal remembrances and anecdotes from the guests. (Several of the services have specific arrangements to follow to facilitate this.) Usually, the words each person speaks are brief, but personal and touching. You might want to arrange in advance for two or three persons to speak, thereby "breaking the ice" and encouraging others. You will have to determine when no one else wants to speak, but be careful not to end this period too soon.

2. You, or another appropriate person (or persons) at your request, can offer a very personal remembrance of the deceased. Often this is done by a son or daughter on behalf of the whole family. If you take on this task, you will be drawing from your own information and memories. Such a eulogy usually lasts from five to ten minutes.

3. You can also gather information from close family members and friends of the deceased and weave that information into a moving and wonderful sketch of the woman or man whose life touched many lives.

This third possibility may seem forbidding. You may think, "How can I possibly gather information and arrange it into a speech in just a few hours, especially in the midst of all the arrangements and distress that are taking place?"

Here is a technique that not only provides you with the necessary information for delivering an outstanding eulogy of the third sort, but it is often the most helpful means for dealing with grief and for beginning the process of healing. The technique has the following steps:

- assemble the immediate family and other appropriate people with the explicit intent of helping you gather information;
- arrange a comfortable setting where you can sit together in an informal circle;
- at the gathering, state clearly that your need is for information and anecdotes about the deceased's life so you can present a eulogy;
- see yourself as the group's facilitator, keeping the conversation flowing;
- encourage everyone to participate;
- do not censor in any way what anyone says;
- take notes on everything said;
- ask questions or give prompts that encourage the people talking to develop their remembrances;
- do not rush to fill the moments of silence.

Such a gathering follows a predictable pattern. The words are hesitant at first, but then the remembrances and anecdotes start to piggyback. Soon the whole group is engaged and animated by the spirit of the deceased and the spirit of love for one another. For those who were more close to the deceased, this can prove to be a most private and satisfying memorial service—even more valuable than the public service to follow.

Later, when you have reviewed your notes and are ready to begin writing a eulogy, look for patterns, key phrases, and characterizations that capture the essence of the individual. Flag anecdotes, especially those that are touching and amusing. You will want to incorporate these into your biographical sketch. *Sketch* is the proper way to view your task of writing a eulogy because you cannot possibly relate all the events of the deceased's life. Instead, you will want to expand on a few themes that developed naturally in conversation with the deceased's family and intimates. Do not attempt to sanitize the deceased's life. Idiosyncrasies and even negative traits can be addressed, if done with sensitivity and in the spirit of love and healing.

Begin writing. You will be suprised how your notes, revealing a theme or several themes, will flow into a moving narrative. The following examples of actual eulogies will show you some ways of arranging information and anecdotes.

A Feisty Woman

Her name was Belle. She was born eighty years ago. She died this week. She had an eventful span of four score years, but eventful only in "ordinary" ways.

When she was three, her mother died. When she was twelve, her father died. She lived with an older sister until she was sixteen and got her first job. It was the Jazz Age, the 1920s, and she learned to smoke cigarettes—a lifelong habit.

By the age of eighteen she married. The marriage didn't work. Belle took her two young children, Betty and Bob, from Gary to Valparaiso and provided for them by working in a hotel laundry. These sparse years in the midst of the Great Depression were hardly a favorable time for a single woman to support a family. But Belle was independent and inwardly tough. Though help was offered her, she knew she could hold her family together and she did.

She remarried. Wally was a good young man—scholarly, warm, and patient. He was the love of her life. They moved to Chicago where they were happy. Wally and Belle even dreamed that someday they could open a flower shop. That someday never came, because Wally was killed in the Second World War. Though crushed, Belle kept her grief contained within herself.

Belle put her life together again. She saw her two children graduate from the Illinois Institute of Technology. And she eventually remarried. She and her new husband Al had a little house on a big lot in Worth. Belle loved her garden. Then Al died. Belle continued her life.

She loved her six grandchildren and they loved her. She gardened and generally enjoyed life. She became a self-appointed coordinator of events and communication that kept her four sisters and herself in closer touch than they had ever been before.

Those are the bare bones of Belle's life—her eighty years.

Let it be known that Belle said she didn't want a funeral or memorial service. She even told her daughter Betty not to bother to pick up her ashes. She meant it. But then again, that comment has a touch of her customary humor about it. Probably she didn't want to make a fuss. Certainly she didn't want family and friends to mourn her death—to grieve for her sake. Life is for living, not grieving, Belle believed. I suspect that she couldn't imagine what might be said about her life: It was so ordinary, so unremarkable.

Well, though there is some grief, it is the spirit of Life that you—her family and friends—feel most this afternoon as you gather to honor her memory. And there is much to be said that is truly remarkable, truly admirable about Belle. Obviously, there are the misfortunes of her life that never seemed to overwhelm her. She was like an accomplished swimmer in the surf—riding through, over, and occasionally buffeted by the waves. The swim was all that more invigorating. She had strength *somewhere* in her small body. It was the strength of outlook and attitude: she never felt sorry for her situation; never conveyed to her children that they were not well off; never clung to hurts or kept grudges. Always there bubbled forth her wonderful sense of humor. Belle always laughed with and never laughed at; hers was a gentle, warm humor. Belle's humor was a trait passed through the generations. I have seen that touch of loving humor in her daughter and in her grandchildren. (The good of a person's life does endure. It lives through love and those who have been touched by love. Love never ends.) It is Belle's attitude—her essential self lived through a gentle life of strength, courage, and will—that will survive through time in her children, grandchildren, and I suspect deeper into future generations. Belle is a fountainhead, a true matriarch.

Belle was a character, too. The world doesn't have enough characters of Belle's quality.

- Money burned a hole in her pocket. When her children were very young, with a bonus check she bought a car. But she didn't know how to drive! She set off from Gary to Detroit. And she wrecked the car.
- When Wally, the children, and she were living in Chicago, she once gave up an apartment rather than a dog, though they did not know where they would sleep the next day.
- Her current dog was always her last dog. But of course it wasn't.

- While she could remember the names of her grandchildren's dogs, she couldn't recall the names of their spouses.
- When she visited, she might stop to pinch off dead buds and flowers and pull a few weeds before ringing the doorbell.
- She always smoked.
- She drove until a few months ago.
- She was an original, though unintentional, feminist; that is, she did things that women didn't generally do, which means she did pretty much what she wanted and was able to do.

For Belle, Life was for the living—as fully as possible, which she did with grace and style and feistiness. We shall miss her. But we are so much more for her having lived.

Salt of the Earth

The philosopher George Santayana wrote, "When a man's life is over, it remains true that he was one sort of man and not another.

"A man who understands himself under the form of eternity knows the quality that eternally belongs to him, and knows that he cannot wholly die, even if he would, for when the movement of his life is over, the truth of his life remains."

Think of Bob in this way. What is the truth of his life that remains? I have considered what might possibly be called the several truths of his life.

There is the truth of *adventure*. He learned as a young boy to wander the countryside with his dog, looking for adventure. Throughout his life he was forever and always seeking adventure. He was a purist fly-fisherman who always kept a pair of waders in his car trunk, ready to wander up any likely stream. He was also a spectacularly unsuccessful fisherman, because he quested to pull fish out of places where they had never been found before. As a result he rarely caught anything.

His family remembers vacation trips when they were never lost, though they had wandered into unknown territory, because Bob would say they were just having another adventure. He would never take the same route home that he had traveled in getting somewhere.

As a teacher he sought to make education an adventure for his students. (You all know how he felt about administrators. He tried it out for himself for a while and declared that he didn't want to count paper clips the rest of his professional career.) The notorious summer camp of the late sixties he helped found, A. Frogg's Place, was an adventure in education. On an old farm on the

Fermi Lab property, delinquents from the Du Page School, hippie counselors, and children of unsuspecting friends enjoyed a free-form summer that brings warm smiles and a hundred stories to those who were a part.

And there is the truth of his *compassion and generosity*. As a boy he had seen Norman Thomas campaign from a front porch in his hometown of Wheaton. His parents were sympathetic to the union movement. During his college years (actually when he was at Roosevelt College getting his under-graduate degree—you see, he also made a lifelong adventure of going to college, many colleges), he worked to get Harold Washington a break-through job with the Chicago Transit Authority. Their strategy kind of backfired, though. Washington got the job but felt compelled to keep it a year—a year longer than he wished. The ACLU, Fair Housing, NAACP, and the Downers Grove Library were among the movements and projects that Bob supported. Through-out his life any program for civil or human rights got his support of time, energy, and money. Because he believed in the Democratic Party's ability to make a more just society, he was a diligent party worker. He toiled to bring the Democratic candidate 33 percent of the Du Page vote—33 being the magic number for election of state candidates. Because Du Page County was over-whelmingly Republican, there were no rewards to come Bob's way. He truly worked for the cause and not for personal reward.

What better measure of his commitment to people than his ease and success with people of all backgrounds and standing?

And there is the truth of *family*. A restless spirit longing for adventure, he nevertheless married and raised two sons. The deep and abiding affection of his wife Tinker (Bob, she says, was gallant, courageous, generous, loving) and of his sons, Miles and Matthew, testifies to this truth better than any word can say. And they knew him in his moods and eccentricities, his shortcomings and failures, through all his rambling, nonlinear, confusing stories. He could infuri-ate those who lived with him. To his family he was *wonderfully* human. He wasn't a hero, bigger than life. He was flawed and lovable, Bob. (We should all be so flawed, so lovable.)

These are truths about Bob, yes, that are eternal. Still they don't express the real truth of the man—the spirit that will be so sorely missed but that lives through his unextinguishable spirit. He was much richer, more complex than just these truths of adventure, compassion, generosity, and family. For those who knew him and loved him the best, he was the *salt of the earth*.

Think about this metaphor for a moment—salt of the earth. I didn't really understand it until I applied it to Bob.

Think about a handful of salt—put your tongue to it; there's bitterness. Bob had a quality of that bitterness. But sprinkle a little salt on food and it makes that food more savory. Bob made life more savory. He was fun, he was good to have around. When you can't have salt, there is nothing more precious. Bob was the *salt of the earth*.

Now, that salt is dissolved in the ocean of life that contains us all. Though we shall miss the gifts of the garden he tended, the stories he would confuse us with, the meandering paths he took us on that led to memorable adventures—the savor he brought to us stays with us. And we are glad he lived and was the man he was.

There is a Jewish saying that God created humankind because God loved stories. Well, if that God and Bob ever meet and Bob tells one of his characteristic, meandering, nonlinear stores, well, I just don't know. . . .

Running, But Not
Running Away

Marion died too soon. She did not want to die, though cancer had spread throughout her body, though she was in tremendous pain.

On her birthday last November, she declared at the end of a "good" day, "God, I want to go on living!" In early January, after a "bad" day, she nevertheless declared, "I must be strong. We will make it work, if I can (and I will) resolve to put all my energy into this effort." The final entry in her calico-covered diary in which she made lists and wrote a few notes about her illness was a notation for a book: *The McDougall Plan for Super Health and Lifelong Weight Loss*. The entry was not dated but was obviously written after January 31, just a half-dozen days ago. Marion was obviously still thinking she could make it work. Her will was still strong. She was looking toward super health and a long life. She died too soon herself, too soon for her family and friends.

She was 48—in the prime of her life, in the midst of truly good, fulfilling years. She died too soon because she was enjoying the honestly earned fruits of her strivings. She died too soon because she had much to do, especially she realized in her last months, in her relationships with family and friends. But she had also accomplished a lot already.

Ten years ago, approaching mid-life, she experienced what many women now experience: a dulling routine; being taken for granted; a certain restlessness to get on with her life; a yearning to test herself and push back the boundaries she had unthinkingly accepted for too long, to discover and explore, to live her life as a favorite poster of hers recommended—"to do my thing; I am not in this world to live up to your expectations. . . . [Y]ou are you and I am I. . . ." She wanted to find her identity and worth.

So she set her goals and began to accomplish them one step at a time: first an exploratory college semester, then full enrollment in a degree program; 4 1/2 years later a degree, followed by a job that was entry level but that in a few years led to the responsibilities of setting up a division and supervising an office of forty workers.

Throughout this personal transformation she was determined, positive, assertive, and deliberate. How she accomplished her remarkable change, I think, is revealed in an anecdote her family remembers vividly.

Marion was a jogger. Every other day she ran five miles. Occasionally she ran a race. After one race, her daughter Sue jauntily said, "I'll run with you next year," thinking of course her mother would forget. A year is a long time to remember such an offhanded remark. Right? Wrong! As the intervening year drew to a close, Sue got a call at school from her mother reminding her that the date they had made to race together was approaching. They did run together, Marion running to the music of her Walkman. Sue flagged badly after the first mile. Marion slowed, encouraged Sue with laughter, advising her to break down the remaining miles into achievable small bits, proceeding from landmark to landmark. She would sight a landmark ahead, telling Sue to just make it to there; then there would be another and then another landmark to reach. Together they crossed the finish line. After the race, Marion told her sister, "Sue would have hated herself if she hadn't finished."

This anecdote tells a lot. First of all Marion was well conditioned. She had natural abilities and she worked to use them to advantage. She enjoyed the competition—the striving and the success. She could have raced ahead, but she chose instead to both run the race and encourage her family. She slowed down so she would not outdistance them. Marion arranged her life into manageable pieces. The little goals along the way were rewarding, and they were also the way to attain the big goals at the end of the race. (One of her favorite posters read, "The race is not always to the swift, but to those who keep running.") Until the very end of her life she kept running toward the big goal of winning. She imparted the wisdom she had acquired through her own strivings to her children. That was important to her, especially in the weeks before her death. She called each of her children individually to her; and, in a sense, they ran together one more time—Marion pointing out the landmarks ahead, the achievable goals—while helping to focus her children's sights on the big goals at the end.

Until her painful, debilitated death, Marion was true to the new self she had made herself into a decade ago.

We shall miss her as an exemplar, an inspiration, because she showed us the way; and we admired her will and courage and dedication. But we shall miss her more because, while she could have outdistanced us as she ran toward her own personal goals, she slowed down to run alongside us, giving encouragement, wise counsel, her wit and laughter, and of course, her love.

The poet Yevgeny Yevtushenko wrote, "Not people die but worlds die in them. . . . They perish. They cannot be brought back. The secret worlds are not regenerated."

Those who were closest to Marion—family, friends, coworkers—know the world that is gone from them because of her death: the concerned, involved, easy, smiling presence; the friendly and responsive ear; the sense of humor; the encouragement and sometimes cajoling urging—she was great at signing people up, getting them involved—the deep and steady determination; the woman still becoming. (In her final month, she began to work on what she called her spiritual side, a dimension she felt she had been neglecting in the quest to succeed.)

But this is not to say she wasn't a woman of spiritual feeling and personal faith. Her God, she discovered, lived within her. For instance, when she ran on Sunday mornings while watching others going off to their churches, she experienced her own spiritual high, the mystic identity between herself and Life. I suspect her God was a realistic God fully shaped and vital, including the vital reality of pain and suffering, of a consciousness of acute sensitivity and mindfulness. For those attributes describe Marion.

And as Yevtushenko says, "We make our lament against that destruction." But we also rejoice in the woman she was—wife, mother, daughter, sister, friend, coworker.

Though we shall miss her, our grief is soothed by the richness of our living memories and her enduring presence in those she touched.

An Excellent Minute, A Tragic Minute

In thinking of John, the life he lived, the sort of person he was, I am reminded of a poem "People" by the poet Yevgeny Yevtushenko:

> To each his world is private,
> And in the world one excellent minute.
> And in that world one tragic minute,
> These are private.
>
> Not people die
> But worlds die in them.

John's life was private, exceedingly private, especially in the sense that you or I could never fully understand what he endured and suffered within the world of his own being during the last years of his life. We saw how his life touched ours and knew how his behavior shaped our private worlds. We knew the orbit of his life, but not the world that was private to him. Though we sought to understand, we didn't really understand what he suffered. The puzzling source of his illness and the inner pain of his depression and compulsive behavior eluded us. Many of his ways were foreign to our ways. So for those who knew John most intimately, there was often frustration and sometimes anger. His stubborn willfulness and his inability to get on with things could confuse and distress us—again and again over many years.

I say these things to speak truthfully of John's ways, to highlight his private world, as inaccessible as it might be. He was a man whose struggles were largely inward, yet who tried to hold to life in the outer world, particularly through relationships with Louise his wife, and his four children, with a persistent and even tenacious courage.

There was always a part of John that was aware, but more than aware, that acted from instincts of compassion and love. When there was acrimony in the family—and there was acrimony—John usually found the means to take the initiative in reconciliation. And there were always those touching and ingratiating displays of his attentiveness, interest, and concern. For instance, if there was a good sale on stepladders (or fire extinguishers or toolboxes), he would buy one for each of his adult children.

And during these difficult later years, there was a part of John that was proud. Though he could no longer hold a job, he did manage the family finances. He kept track of a growth-oriented investment portfolio that returned dividends equivalent to a fair salary. Thus, John was able, in his own way, to contribute to the welfare of the family. And by this he achieved a sense of self-worth and dignity.

During his final year, from November until his death a week ago, when his health had declined precipitously, John made a special effort to reach out to his family. He was less defensive, more vulnerable. This was ingratiating and sad. (We might imagine from this something of the constant strain he put himself through for years to maintain appearances.) In the final months he was making arrangements to turn over financial management affairs to his sons. His eldest daughter, Jeanne, and he had a memorable time at a Marvin Hamlisch concert in April. During a set portion of Hamlisch's concert, John shouted out a song title, something along the lines of "Why Are You Going Through the Contents of My Garbage Can?", which Hamlisch and the audience delighted in.

So, in his final months, John tried to reach out from his private world to his family. They knew this and were touched by his intentions, though they were no less exasperated by his eccentricities and annoyances.

In the sense that this latter part of his life cannot be forgotten, we also remember his earlier days. The difficult years are measured against memories of happier times. And at such a time as this, when death winnows out the darker days of a man's life, there are gracious days to recall. And isn't it wonderful how strong and persistent these positive recollections are? And isn't it amazing how this sifting reveals true and deep feelings—leading to the power and affirmation of love?

Now we recall that John was a devoted son to a mother who told him that he should get married, no matter how comfortable he was at home. And when he married Louise, he never had any doubt who came first in his life.

Now we recall that John was an active volunteer. He served his professional society in a variety of capacities. He helped raise money for his church and the Y. He was involved in Indian Guides when his children were young. He organized block parties.

Now we recall that John and Louise were indefatigable vacationers, packing their kids and gear in a station wagon, trekking to Glacier, Mesa Verde, Yellowstone, and other such great American vacation spots.

Now we recall that John was a shutterbug for whom no event was official without it being recorded forever on film. His children mused that a fitting memorial service would be to show you all the slides John ever took!

Now we recall that John was proud of his role as father to his four children. Indeed, among the losses of his life, losing his children as they grew up was among the hardest for him to adjust to and bear.

His family agrees: John will be with them forever, even when they won't want him to be there. John, who taught them by early example, is in his children's sure and strong values. And he is in their frustrations, too.

Which is to say, memories of him are rich with ambivalence.

His children remember him as a tough and demanding task-master who gave tedious instructions and was irritatingly vigilant in their cutting of the grass. And they remember him for the airplane rides—swinging them through the air by their arms.

He told awful, corny jokes that inevitably evoked groans. He was also predictably late for family events.

He was John, who desperately wanted to be a normal Joe and who always had the best intention no matter how faulty his execution. He was John, in the final analysis, a living and compassionate man whose wife and children have measured the sorrows and joys he gave them and who say without reservation, "We shall miss him."

And with this sense of our loss, we make our lament against the destruction of his life.

Food and Socializing

Although the formal service is the main event, it is not the only component of what might be called "good grief." Usually, on the day before or sometimes just before the service, there is a set time to visit the deceased's family and perhaps view the body "in state." It is equally, if not more, important to have a gathering after the service and interment.

Such a gathering provides a valuable opportunity to socialize and eat. While this may seem a burden on the close family, they will find a heartening reservoir of strength from the mere presence of their family and friends. And they will welcome the opportunity to greet the attendees and benefit from the condolences of those who have come to show their respect.

Socializing and eating have other benefits to recommend holding a reception after the formal service. Those who have attended the formal service will have pent-up emotions and unspoken expressions. Friends will have the opportunity to express their own sense of loss as well as offer each other condolences. Introductions and renewed acquaintances will make real the web of connections woven through the life of the deceased. And just being together demonstrates the affirmation that life continues and the human community survives every death.

Food at such an occasion becomes communion with Life, again affirming that life and community survive. Food also helps fill the emptiness—a physical manifestation of the loss. It allows for family and friends to do something concrete and helpful—by bringing food and by pitching in to serve or clean up. Also, in a concrete way the family can thank those who attended by offering hospitality. And food is a good "excuse" to gather people together.

Depending on the setting and circumstances, this important conclusion to the public mourning process takes a variety of forms. Here are some possibilities.

- It can be a simple beverage and finger-food affair in another room of the funeral home, church, or hall. Or it might be a sit-down dinner or a more substantial buffet arranged on behalf of or by the family.
- The reception is most commonly held in the family home with a buffet table watched over by family, friends, or neighbors, often with food brought by these people and others who want to be of service. Or it can be a catered buffet provided by the family.
- The reception can be held in a restaurant, usually in a private room arranged for in advance with food prepared and served by the restaurant's staff. This is a relatively expensive alternative but may suit certain circumstances best.

It does not matter how elaborate or how simple this conclusion to the day's event is. What matters is the opportunity for all concerned to get together in a friendly, intimate way. You will not want to neglect this instinctive and time-honored practice, because it is both a winding down and a starting over on the most personal level for those most intimately involved with the deceased and the deceased's family.

Rituals of Remembrance

Effective grieving results in a return to relative normality—living a reconstructed life in the absence of the deceased. Within such a reconstructed life, it is spiritual and therapeutic to remember and honor the deceased, especially through acts that are small and natural rituals, often at a site where remains have been buried or scattered. Think about such a site as you preplan for yourself or deal with the immediate needs of a death.

The growing popularity of cremation combined with a long-standing cultural denial of death have made it all to easy to neglect the importance of tangible memorials, including traditional interment and the subsequent erection of a monument. In this regard, having a place to physically visit and perform small, natural rituals of remembrance has ongoing value.

After cremation, interment is frequently postponed for weeks, months, even years. Sometimes the box or urn of ashes is literally put out of sight in a closet or even the trunk of a car, but it is not put out of mind. The survivors cannot bring themselves to dispose of the ashes, yet they do not know how to do so effectively. When the remains are finally buried, survivors usually have a sense of relief and take comfort in visiting the grave or other site where the ashes have been interred or scattered.

I recently officiated at the interment of the ashes of a vital and beautiful woman, only twenty-six years old, who had died a few months earlier. It was a moody late September afternoon, warm and humid. The setting was a gem of a small cemetery set apart from the contemporary sprawl of a Chicago suburb. Her husband and young stepson, mother and father, brother and sister-in-law, and a few close friends met me by the front gates. We decided to walk to the grave, following a winding strip of macadam down a small hill, past a serene pond. Though we had not intended it to be so, we made a procession. The husband carried an armful of roses, the stepson the urn of ashes, friends small bouquets. The mother and father, arm in arm, supported each other.

We were all aware of nature's embrace: the great old oak and maple trees arching over us, the geese floating on the water, the crows flying overhead, even the mosquitoes we attracted. The drone of airplanes added a note of contrast.

The ceremony was simple. As I read Edna St. Vincent Millay's "Dirge Without Music," scores of roosting crows stirred and cawed their protests. They rose above the treetops and swirled in agitation—palpable expressions of our grief. The husband lowered the ashes into the ground and crumbled dirt over the urn, as did others. He lovingly slid the temporary cover over it, covering the wound with the flowers. We admired the gravestone etched with a Celtic cross and a garland of primroses. I was sure that everyone present felt, as I felt, incredibly embedded in reality. We experienced realizations too great for words.

We had held an emotional and satisfying memorial service three months earlier, but this humble interment had even more impact on this core group of intimate family and friends because of the finality. There were still bitter tears. But because of the finality, everyone now had permission to move on. There was nothing left undone. In that natural place of perpetual repose, her family had dedicated her remains to the keeping of a hallowed place. They vowed with their secret selves silently and with one another out loud that they would return to her grave to revive her memory and even commune with her.

We retraced the way we had arrived—relieved of a burden we had carried in with us and had left to the keeping of nature and eternity. We lingered by the gate, reluctant to end this poignant, meaningful moment.

Rituals of remembrance often include a yearly schedule of visits combined with a floral tribute. Birth or death anniversaries, mothers' and fathers' days, Easter, Thanksgiving, and Memorial Day are common dates to visit graves.

There is a lingering custom that a return to one's family home, for instance, at a holiday, begins with—or at least includes—"paying respects" to family graves, often with a floral tribute. This not only shows respect but promotes a sense of continuity and involvement. A sacred responsibility, it offers a tacit promise to all persons that they will not be forgotten after death. It is a loving act that is also therapeutic. Once the duty is ritually fulfilled, the survivors have permission to get on with their lives.

It is possible to honor a beloved's request to scatter ashes, perhaps in a favorite natural setting, while erecting a suitable monument in a cemetery or other appropriate place elsewhere so the survivors will have a place to visit, remember the deceased, and contemplate their own mortality. Some persons go so far as to choose or write their own epithet—a phrase carved in stone—as a summary of their life or as an ongoing message to the living.

Living Memorials

You might also consider the value of all sorts of living or continuing memorials—tangible remembrances that are also generally useful in long-term grief work and rituals of remembrance for the survivors. Nature, the arts, education, charities, and philanthropies are common areas of designated memorial gifts.

Many persons favor the planting of a tree or some other sort of planting in a public space—a churchyard, park, arboretum, community garden. Benches, fountains, ponds, and accessible walkways are some of the possibilities for associating the deceased with nature or appreciation of nature. Among the most useful of cemetery memorials are permanent stone benches. Many organizations offer more modest but enduring memorials such as an inscribed brick in a garden walkway or patio or a shrub or tree incorporated into a landscape.

Works of art—painting or sculptures—given to beautify public space are common memorials. For those who love music and have the means, a piano given to a church or school has special significance. Appropriate books donated to a library, inscribed with a dedication to the deceased, are inexpensive but valuable memorials.

Endowed scholarships or donations to designated scholarship funds continue avocations and professions by educating future generations. Many, in gratitude to their alma maters, leave memorial bequests to their undergraduate and graduate universities, where their money increases other endowed funds. Charities and philanthropies are frequent recipients of memorial gifts. The church of the deceased heads this list. Surviving families often request that memorial tributes be sent to an organization that researches the illness of or care for the terminally ill, such as the American Cancer Society, the American Heart Association, or a local hospice.

There is wisdom in designating a suitable memorial well in advance of death. A living memorial is a ritual of remembrance because it is tangible, ongoing, and useful. The more intimate or closely associated it is with the deceased, the more powerful it will be in serving the survivors in the process of grief and recovery. A just proportion of your estate—possibly the traditional tithe—is your final gift of gratitude to the world, humanity, and culture that sustained you throughout your life. While there are instances when anonymity has its place, do not discount your desire not to be forgotten or to continue to contribute to our common world. We all want to be remembered, especially for being loving and giving: a person of true charity. It is best to plan this or leave instructions rather than to leave it up to your survivors, who may be overwhelmed by the immediacy of events and the shocking grief of death.

Survivors can use these suggestions to determine appropriate and lasting living memorials that will be focal points of continuing rituals of remembrance. Gifts to such relatively permanent memorials may be requested in lieu of flowers at the time of death.

Appendix A:
Personal Plans and Arrangements

Name _____

Address _____

_____

_____

Phone _____

Social Security # _____

Attorney and address _____

_____

Location of will _____

Location of living will _____

Durable power of Attorney for health care given to (name and address):

_____

_____

Other special arrangements _____

_____

_____

_____

_____

_____

Next of kin and address _____

_____

_____

Family members to contact _____

_____

_____

_____

Church affiliation _____

_____

Affiliations and organizations _____

_____

_____

Memorial gifts in my memory should be sent to _____

_____

_____

_____

If appropriate, provide the following information.

Preferred funeral home _____

_____

Memorial society _____

_____

Cemetery lot _____

_____

Organ donation _____

_____

Body to medical school_____

_____

Circle preferences:

1)   funeral   memorial service   graveside   no service

2)   visitation   no visitation

3)   open casket   closed casket

4)   direct cremation   cremation after funeral

5)   burial of body   burial of cremains

6)   mausoleum   niche

7)   scattering of ashes   Where? _____

_____

_____

Further instructions and arrangements _____

_____

_____

_____

_____

_____

_____

_____

Copies of this document should be (1) filed with your minister and your attorney, (2) placed with your personal papers, and (3) given to your next of kin for her/his information.

_____

signed   dated

Appendix B:
Writing an
Obituary

If you want to assure that you'll be accurately remembered, write your own obituary! Not only will this assure accuracy, you will relieve your survivors of a necessary task—gathering and organizing information—during a tumultuous time.

A bonus: you'll find writing your own obituary a reflective exercise of self-discovery.

Here's an outline that follows a format consistent with standard journalistic practice:

1. Fill out the accompanying form "Personal History for My Obituary" to organize your information.

2. The opening paragraph contains basic information: your name, your occupation and/or primary identity, your residence, your age. For example: "Jane Smith, a life-long resident of Middletown and a retired teacher, died on _____ at _____. Mrs. Smith was _____ years old."

3. The next two or three paragraphs summarize the highlights and activities of your life. Mention your occupation or business, the professional and voluntary organizations to which you belong, military service, your church or temple, and club, fraternal, service, or other affiliations. Include your special accomplishments as well as your special interests and involvements. Don't be shy!

4. Include any voluntary or civic offices held and awards received.

5. In the next to last paragraph list your immediate survivors, their relationships to you, and their hometowns.

6. The final paragraph will, upon your death, tell of funeral arrangements. If appropriate, include whether you request charitable contributions in lieu of flowers to the charities of your choice.

7. Type your final draft, double-spaced, on 8.5 by 11-inch white paper. A page—a page and a half at most—is the right length.

Finally, compile a list with addresses of publications you want to receive your obituary. In addition to your local newspaper, you might want to include newspapers in areas where you formerly lived. For this purpose you can target your obituary by localizing the opening paragraph. "Jane Smith, a former resident of Centerville, died on _____ in Middletown, where she had lived for the last twenty years." In your list include fraternal, alumni, and professional journals you want notified. Append this list to your obituary. Make copies and give them to your attorney, next of kin, and clergy, and leave a set with your personal papers.

Appendix C:
Personal History
for Obituary

Name _____

Date of birth _____

Place of birth _____

Mother's name _____

and birthplace _____

Father's name _____

and birthplace _____

Marital status:　☐ single　　☐ married　　☐ widowed　　☐ divorced

☐ other _____

Spouse's name _____

Date of marriage _____

Place of marriage _____

Children's names and years of birth _____

_____

_____

Brothers and sisters _____

_____

_____

_____

Occupation(s) and employment _____

_____

_____

_____

_____

_____

_____

_____

Education (school, year, degree) _____

Military service (years and rank) _____

_____

_____

_____

Organizations and memberships _____

_____

_____

_____

Awards, honors, special achievements _____

_____

_____

_____

Other information _____

_____

_____

_____